John Quincy Adams

6th President of
the United States

John Quincy Adams was a superb secretary of state but an ineffective chief executive. After his retirement from the presidency, he served for 17 years in Congress, where he fought for the right of petition and for the liberty of black slaves. (Library of Congress.)

John Quincy Adams

6th President of the United States

Miriam Greenblatt

GARRETT EDUCATIONAL CORPORATION

Cover: *Official presidential portrait of John Quincy Adams by George P. A. Healy.* (Copyrighted by the White House Historical Association; photograph by the National Geographic Society.)

Edited and produced by Synthegraphics Corporation

Library of Congress Cataloging in Publication Data

Greenblatt, Miriam.
John Quincy Adams, 6th President of the United States/ Miriam Greenblatt.
   p.   cm. – (Presidents of the United States)
Includes bibliographical references.
Summary: Presents the life of John Quincy Adams, including his childhood, education, employment, and political career.
   1. Adams, John Quincy, 1767–1848 – Juvenile literature. 2. Presidents – United States – Biography – Juvenile literature. 3. United States – Politics and government – 1825–1829 – Juvenile literature. 4. United States – Foreign relations – 1783–1865 – Juvenile literature. [1. Adams, John Quincy, 1767–1848. 2. Presidents.] I. Title. II. Series.
E377.G74   1990
973.5′5′092 – dc20
[B]
[92]
ISBN 0-944483-21-6
                      89-39950
                      CIP
                      AC

Contents

Chronology for
John Quincy Adams

1767 Born on July 11 in Braintree, Massachusetts

1778– Lived mostly in Europe and attended
1785 schools there

1787 Graduated from Harvard College

1790 Began practicing law in Boston

1794 Appointed ambassador to the Netherlands by President George Washington

1797 Married Louisa Johnson on July 26; appointed ambassador to Prussia by President John Adams

1802– Served as a member of the
1803 Massachusetts Senate

1803– Served as a member of the U.S. Senate
1808

1809– Ambassador to Russia
1814

1815– Ambassador to Great Britain
1817

1817– Served as secretary of state under
1825 President James Monroe

1825– Served as 6th President of the
1829 United States

1831– Served as a member of the U.S. House
1848 of Representatives

1848 Died on February 23 in Washington, D.C.

Chapter 1

Early Years

Eight-year-old John Quincy Adams opened his eyes. A pale pre-dawn light shone through his bedroom window. Quickly he looked around the room, not quite certain what had awakened him. Then it came again—a dull, rolling sound like distant thunder.

With a start, John Quincy jumped from the bed and began pulling on his pants and shirt. In the next room, five-year-old Charles and three-year-old Tommy were anxiously demanding to know what was going on. John Quincy ordered them to stay where they were until he returned. Then, heart pounding, he raced barefoot down the stairs, out of the house, and through the orchard to nearby Penn's Hill. From the rocky ledge on top, one could see the nearby city and harbor of Boston through a spyglass.

John Quincy knew it wasn't thunder that had awakened him. It was the sound of booming cannon. On June 17, 1775, such a sound meant only one thing. Full-scale war had broken out between the 13 American colonies and England!

John Quincy spent most of the day in his front-row seat observing the Battle of Bunker Hill. He saw the red flares of the guns on the decks of the British warships as they hurled volley after volley at the American fort. He watched the gray

The battle of Bunker Hill was actually fought on nearby Breed's Hill in Charlestown. The mistake was made by the first newspaper accounts of the battle. The Americans lost 400 men, the British lost 1,000 men. (Library of Congress.)

smoke from fires drift along the bay. In the late afternoon, he carried water to passing soldiers and refugees. And in the evening, he and his brothers and sister sat in the kitchen while their mother taught them a poem in honor of Scottish warriors who had died fighting the British in 1745. From that day on, every morning when he got up, John Quincy would recite first the Lord's Prayer and then the poem to fallen warriors.

The Battle of Bunker Hill symbolized many of the principles our nation's sixth president was to follow all his life. First, it was a battle—and John Quincy Adams had a fighting spirit that would not be subdued, although he used words instead of guns. Second, it helped create a nation—and John Quincy Adams later helped defend that nation against foreign enemies, sectional divisions, and party politics alike. Most important of all, its goal was liberty—and from his election to Congress at the age of 63 until his death at 80, John Quincy Adams waged an unending battle for the liberty of black slaves.

THE ILLUSTRIOUS ADAMS FAMILY

John Quincy Adams was born on July 11, 1767, in that part of the seacoast town of Braintree that is now Quincy, Massachusetts. Named for his great-grandfather, who was dying when he was born, John Quincy was the second child and the oldest of the three sons of John and Abigail Adams.

Being born an Adams carried a great responsibility. Members of the Adams family had been living in Massachusetts for about 130 years. All had been hard-working, successful farmers. They had also been people of importance in their local communities. John Quincy's great-grandfather,

The birthplace of John Quincy Adams is typical of the kind of house owned by a prosperous lawyer-farmer of the period. (Library of Congress.)

for example, had represented Braintree in the Massachusetts colonial legislature for 40 years and had served as Speaker of the House for much of that time. John Quincy's father had attended Harvard College and had become a successful lawyer. Abigail Adams was the daughter of a Congregational minister, a highly respected profession in a colony founded by religious people. So naturally, a great deal was expected of John Quincy.

Two Houses

The first few years of John Quincy's life were spent alternating between Braintree and Boston, nine miles away. In Braintree, the family lived in a typical New England saltbox-style house. It had a huge central chimney and a sloping roof that shed snow easily. There were four rooms on the first floor, three bedrooms across the front upstairs, and, in the rear, an open space under the rafters called a "leanter." The house was made of wood, and only the living room and the kitchen were heated. In winter, when John Quincy went to bed, he took along a warming pan to remove the chill from the bedclothes. Almost none of the furniture matched, and there were no closets for hanging clothes, just pegs driven into the walls. The house had no bathroom, and water for cooking and washing came from an outdoor well.

The Adamses had a much grander house in Boston. A three-story building finished on the outside in white brick, it stood on Brattle Square, near the city's busy docks and bustling markets. John Quincy and his older sister, Nabby, often played hide-and-go-seek in its many rooms and along its curving hallways. They also played in the walled garden behind the house.

A CHILD OF THE REVOLUTION

From the time of his birth, John Quincy's life was caught up in the growing rebellion by American colonists against their British overseers. The trouble had started in 1763, at the end of the conflict known in America as the French and Indian Wars. Although the British won this war against France, the English government found itself almost bankrupt. Because it had spent huge sums to equip its armies and send them overseas, the English government decided to tax its American colonies. The action seemed reasonable because the war had freed the colonies from fear of attack by France's Indian allies.

The colonists saw things differently, however. For 150 years they had been managing their own affairs under their colonial charters. They believed they were entitled to the same political rights as English people. But because Americans were not represented in Parliament (the English legislature), they felt that Parliament had no right to tax them. "No taxation without representation!" was the cry heard throughout the 13 colonies.

The first attempt by the English government to raise money in the colonies was the Stamp Act of 1765. A tax on newspapers and legal documents, it was repealed the following year after Americans refused to buy British goods. In 1767, just 12 days before John Quincy was born, the English government tried again. The Townshend Acts levied duties (taxes) on various products imported into the colonies. Again the Americans resisted. This time the English government responded by sending 1,500 redcoats, as the British soldiers were called, to Boston to make sure the tax laws were obeyed.

Even when he was past 60, President John Quincy Adams enjoyed telling visitors to the White House about the time his cousin Sam Adams had taken him to see the redcoats. They were a dazzling sight for the two-year-old boy. Each soldier wore a scarlet greatcoat with shiny brass buttons and white trimmings. His gaiters, or leggings, had been put on wet so that they clung tightly to his legs. He wore his hair with stiff curls on either side and a long tail in back.

John Quincy admired "the pretty redcoats" as the long line of British soldiers moved forward to the swirl of fifes and the rattle of drums. Cousin Sam, however, called them "dreadful redcoats." To Sam Adams, as to John Adams, the redcoats were enemies who must be made to leave America.

Life in Braintree

Over the next several years, John Quincy's father played an increasingly active role in opposing the British. In 1774 he was elected to represent Massachusetts at the First Continental Congress. Since that meant he would be spending most of his time in Philadelphia rather than Boston, he sent his wife and four children to Braintree for safety.

There, Abigail Adams managed the house and the farm. John Quincy helped all he could. He worked with the hired man to plant crops in the spring and harvest them in the fall. He checked the fences to make certain they had not been knocked over by animals. He also drove a cart to nearby pits for gravel and helped his sister do housework and take care of his two younger brothers.

Ordinarily, John Quincy would have attended the grammar school in Braintree, but its one teacher had joined the Continental Army. So John Quincy's early education was supervised by his mother. Every evening after his farm chores were finished, he would sit in the candle-lit kitchen and read aloud. He read books about ancient history and religion. He also read Shakespeare's plays and even tried to read Milton's long poem *Paradise Lost*. If he mispronounced a difficult word, his mother would correct him. The young boy also studied Latin and Greek with one of his father's law clerks who was then living with the family. He mastered Latin quickly but had a great deal of trouble with Greek.

Like most youngsters of the period, John Quincy learned to ride a horse at an early age. When he was nine years old, he became the family's "little post rider." Every day except Sunday he would ride between Braintree and Boston, collecting and delivering the Adams mail. He did this chore for about a year and a half.

A Dangerous Voyage

In February 1778, when he was 10½ years old, John Quincy Adams set out on his first trip to Europe. His father was being sent to Paris by the Continental Congress to help bring France into the Revolutionary War on the side of the United States. The Adamses wanted John Quincy to have the benefits of a European education.

The six-week journey across the Atlantic was exciting but dangerous. The frigate *Boston* was so overloaded with cannon that it pitched and rolled even in fair weather. John Quincy spent much of the time being seasick. On the frigate's first morning out of Massachusetts Bay, it was spotted by several British warships that chased it for two days. No sooner had the *Boston* escaped its pursuers than it was struck by a winter storm. Supplies and furnishings were smashed to bits, and several sailors were injured when a lightning bolt hit the main mast. After three days, the storm finally died down.

The Postal Service

Postal service in the late 1700s was very different from postal service today. For one thing, there were no postage stamps. Instead, the person to whom a letter was addressed paid the postage when he or she received the letter. The usual cost was 25 cents for one sheet of writing and 50 cents for two sheets of writing. However, the price went up if the letter was carried more than 25 miles.

In addition to no stamps, there were no envelopes. People wrote on paper sheets that measured 11 by 14 inches. After the letter was finished, the sheet was folded twice from top to bottom and then twice again from side to side. A blob of sealing wax held the folds of the paper in place. Rich people often pressed the hot wax with a personal seal that was engraved with their name and, usually, some kind of design or motto.

In large cities, letters were delivered to government post offices. In smaller towns or villages, however, letters were left at a store or an inn until they were called for by the addressee.

Until about 1810, people wrote with a quill pen made from the feathers of a goose. After 1810, steel pens gradually came into use.

Next, an English privateer, or pirate ship, began firing at the *Boston*. John Quincy's father just missed being hit. After several hours, American sailors managed to board the enemy ship and force it to surrender. It was then sent back to the United States as a prize of war.

Through it all, John Quincy behaved with great courage. As his father wrote in his diary: "Mr. Johnny's behavior gave me a satisfaction that I cannot express; fully [aware] of our danger, he was constantly endeavoring to bear it with manly patience." John Quincy also did not waste his time. He learned the name and purpose of every sail on the ship and how to read a mariner's compass. He began studying French with three of the French passengers aboard. By the time the *Boston* docked at the port of Bordeaux, John Quincy was able to order his dinner in French.

LIFE IN EUROPE

John Quincy and his father settled in Passy, a suburb of Paris. While John Adams carried on his diplomatic duties, John Quincy attended a private boarding school, studying French, Latin, dancing, drawing, fencing, and music. On weekends he and his father walked the streets of Paris. They toured the Cathedral of Notre Dame and the magnificent palace and gardens at Versailles. In the Bois de Boulogne, a large park, they watched performances of French plays by a company of child actors. John Quincy soon developed a great love for the theater; he also developed a crush on one of the little French actresses.

It was at this time that John Quincy, at his father's suggestion, began keeping a diary. At the top of the first page, he wrote the following statement by the French philosopher Voltaire: *La mollesse est douce et sa suite est cruelle* ("Idleness is sweet but its consequences are cruel"). John Quincy wrote in his diary every day for the rest of his life. It was eventually published in 12 large volumes.

John Adams' assignment in Paris was soon over, and in August 1779 father and son returned to the United States. They had scarcely set foot on American soil when Congress gave the elder Adams another European assignment. This time, John Quincy did not want to go along. He preferred to enter Andover Academy in preparation for attending Harvard College; his goal was to become a lawyer like his father. But Abigail Adams put her foot down. John Quincy enjoyed special advantages as an Adams, she said, so he must take on special responsibilities. He had a "family destiny" to live up to. "Now that you know the French language and are somewhat more mature," Abigail told her son, "you can be helpful to your father in many ways. . . . As for your education . . . you will find the European preparatory schools as good as those in this country." Besides, Abigail pointed out, John Quincy would be learning about diplomacy and foreign affairs first hand.

So John Quincy sailed back to France. His second trip to Europe proved to be "the golden period of his life."

An Education Abroad

In later years, John Quincy Adams wrote in his diary that "I am a man of reserved, cold, austere, and forbidding manners; my political adversaries say, a gloomy [hater of people], and my personal enemies [say], an unsocial savage." As a teenager in Paris, however, John Quincy was a lively, sociable, fun-loving young man. "There is nothing I relish like a good joke," he said. He attended numerous parties, flirted with all his dancing partners, and went drinking with the sons of other diplomats.

After several months in Paris, the Adams family moved

to Amsterdam, in the Netherlands. There John Quincy added Dutch to the languages he spoke. He also spent considerable time in winter skating on the frozen canals.

In 1781, when he was just 14 years old, John Quincy received his first diplomatic assignment. Francis Dana, an old friend of the Adams family, was ordered by Congress to the court of Catherine the Great of Russia. His mission was to persuade the Russian monarch to recognize the United States as an independent nation. Dana needed a secretary who could speak French, the language of international diplomacy. John Adams suggested his son—and John Quincy soon found himself in the Russian capital of St. Petersburg (now Leningrad).

John Quincy spent about 18 months in St. Petersburg. Because Catherine the Great more or less ignored Dana, John Quincy's own official duties were very light. So—as was to be expected—he put his time to good use. He learned German (one of the first Americans to do so) and read one thick history book after another. He also observed and analyzed Russia's government and society. "The nation is composed wholly of nobles and serfs," he wrote his mother, "or, in other words, masters and slaves. . . . This form of government is disadvantageous to the sovereign, to the nobles and to the people. For, first it exposes the sovereign in every moment to revolution, of which there have been already four in the course of this century."

Learning Diplomacy

In October 1782, John Quincy left St. Petersburg to return to the Netherlands. The journey across Europe lasted six months and included stopovers in Copenhagen, Denmark;

Hamburg, Germany; and other large cities. In each, John Quincy observed and analyzed local political and economic conditions, and drafted long reports for his father. John Adams was so impressed that when he was sent to Paris to help negotiate a peace treaty to end the Revolutionary War, he took the 16-year-old John Quincy along as a secretary to the American delegation.

In Paris, John Quincy continued his diplomatic education. He sat in on the discussions between England and its former colonies. He greatly admired Thomas Jefferson, one of the other American delegates, and spent many a long evening with him talking about history, politics, and science. He took several side trips to London, spending hours in the visitors' gallery of the House of Commons listening to the great orators of the day. In later years, when John Quincy was a congressman from Massachusetts, he modeled his speeches after those he had heard in Parliament.

All in all, John Quincy obtained a superb education in foreign affairs. He learned how to negotiate with a diplomatic opponent and the importance of taking a firm stand on basic issues. The one thing he did not learn much about, unfortunately, was how to get along with other people.

Chapter 2

Student, Lawyer, and Pamphleteer

In 1785 John Adams was appointed minister (ambassador) to Great Britain, and 18-year-old John Quincy had to decide whether to accompany his father to London or go home and start his law career. His six years in Europe had been extremely happy, and he could always attend an English university. But he kept remembering his mother's words—that he should become "an ornament to society, an honor to your country, and a blessing to your parents." The only way John Quincy could achieve his mother's ambitions for himself was to become financially independent. It was time to return to the United States.

So once again John Quincy left Europe and went back to his native land. By this time he had reached his full height of five feet, seven inches. He had a plump, somewhat rounded body; thick, curly hair; and a habit of cocking his head to one side, half closing one eye, and sticking his right hand in his pocket. He was very serious-minded and considered himself quite superior to most people. At the same time, he was aware of his shortcomings and worried about them a good deal. Although outwardly calm, he was quick to take offense. He was also extremely opinionated. There was never any doubt as to what John Quincy thought about anything.

A HARVARD MAN

After spending several months brushing up on Greek and mathematics, John Quincy was admitted to Harvard as a junior. Because of his father's position as America's first ambassador to Great Britain, he did not have to pay tuition. Harvard was the oldest of the dozen or so colleges then in existence in the United States. Founded in 1636, it was named after the Reverend John Harvard, who donated half his fortune and a library of some 400 books to the fledgling institution. Harvard's original purpose was to train clergymen. However, in order to meet expenses, it accepted students who did not intend to enter the ministry. (The annual cost of tuition, room, and board was about $100—the same amount that a carpenter earned in a year.)

The curriculum at Harvard emphasized religion, the classics (Latin and Greek literature), moral philosophy, mathematics, and some science. Most instruction was in Latin. The faculty included the president, three professors, and four tutors. Their average age was 24.

John Quincy worked hard at Harvard. He began each day at six o'clock in the morning with prayers in the large hall. Classes ran from eight until twelve. The noonday meal was followed by an athletic period, after which John Quincy retired to his room to study. Like the other 139 undergraduates, he always dressed in a blue-grey uniform of tailcoat, waistcoat, and breeches, with silver buckles on his shoes.

Although he kept himself somewhat aloof from his fellow students, John Quincy had a few friends—"the best characters in my class." With them, he drank cider, smoked, and talked endlessly about books and other serious subjects. Sometimes they would visit a neighboring village in the evening and serenade young ladies under their windows. John

Quincy occasionally accompanied the other young men on his flute.

In 1787 John Quincy graduated from Harvard before an audience filled with "beaming brothers, uncles, aunts and cousins." Since he came in second in his class of 57, he was asked to deliver one of the valedictory addresses. He chose as his topic "Importance and Necessity of Public Faith to the Well-being of a Government." It was a timely subject. The United States was then only six years old, and already there were disagreements between those who favored a stronger national government and those who were satisfied with a weak one. John Quincy's speech was well received. Even the local press made favorable comments about it.

A Lost Love

The way to become a lawyer in 1787 was to read law books in the office of a practicing attorney and then take the bar examination. Accordingly, John Quincy moved to the coastal town of Newburyport and for three years read law in the offices of Theophilus Parsons (who later became Chief Justice of the Massachusetts Supreme Court). He found it very tiresome, for he did not like law. He had chosen to become a lawyer only because it was the quickest way to financial independence.

What John Quincy really wanted to do was write. He filled his diary with sonnets, lyrical descriptions of "the sweet village" of Newburyport, and raw material for what he hoped would one day be "a long and soaring epic in heroic verse."

At the same time, John Quincy was caught up in a social whirl. He went on sleigh rides in winter and sailing parties in summer. He joined a young men's club where the table was always "loaded with big-bellied bottles that made it hard to study law books next morning." He also—for the first and only time in his life—fell deeply in love. Her name was Mary Frazier, a daughter of a former town official of Newburyport. She had blond hair, blue eyes, and a mind "adorned by nature and by art refined." John Quincy poured out his heart to her in verse, took her dancing at Sawyer's Tavern, and serenaded her in public several times. In 1790 he wrote a college chum, "You may know (though it is known to very few) that all my hopes of future happiness in this life center in the possession of that girl."

Unhappily for John Quincy, it was not to be. The Frazier family, although politically prominent, was poor. John Quincy, who by this time had been admitted to the bar and was living in Boston, had high hopes for the future but had very few clients. Abigail Adams wrote several letters to her son reminding him emphatically about the importance of keeping himself "free from entanglements of all kinds" and pointing out that he was being very cruel in maintaining a relationship with Mary "when his situation [does] not permit him to speak."

At last the two young people decided that duty was more important than love. They parted, each promising not to marry someone less worthy than the other. John Quincy, bitterly unhappy, threw himself into his career.

POLITICAL ISSUES

By the 1790s political issues were beginning to divide the United States. One issue had to do with the country's form of government. After six years under the Articles of Confederation, Americans had decided that they needed a stronger national government. The result was the U.S. Constitution. It gave the federal government, rather than the states, control over such matters as interstate commerce, foreign trade, national taxation, a national system of courts, an army, a navy, and what was called "the national welfare." What that phrase actually meant, however, was a matter of great controversy.

A second issue of the times was who should direct the government. Should it be an educated, propertied elite of merchants, planters, lawyers, and clergy, as had been the case so far? Or should the right to vote, and thus political power, be extended to people without property?

A third issue had to do with foreign affairs. Here the question was whether the United States should become involved in the quarrels that were shaking the nations of Europe or whether it should try to maintain a position of neutrality. Many wondered if a policy of neutrality was even possible.

During the Revolutionary War, America's political leaders had been united on the issue of independence from Great Britain. Now they were divided, forming what John Quincy called "internal factions." These factions were soon to develop into full-fledged political parties.

An Angry Essayist

At first John Quincy had no intention of becoming involved in politics. What he wanted was to build up his law practice. But he did not figure on the French Revolution, Tom Paine, or Thomas Jefferson.

The French Revolution began in 1789, when the French people overthrew their monarchy and set up a republic. Soon after, they cut off the head of their former king. Many Americans were horrified. Louis XVI had sent them soldiers, ships, and money to help fight the Revolutionary War. They were shocked even more by the Reign of Terror, under which thousands of French people were guillotined (beheaded) because of their political views.

Despite these excesses, many Americans supported the French Revolution. One of them was Tom Paine. In 1776 his pamphlet *Common Sense* played a large part in convincing Americans to fight for independence. Now Paine wrote another pamphlet called *The Rights of Man*. In it he not only praised the French people for replacing a monarchy with a republic but called on the British to do the same.

If that had been all there was to *The Rights of Man*, John Quincy would probably have done nothing more than discuss the pamphlet at a Saturday night meeting of the Crackbrained Club, a group of young professional men that he had helped to organize. But the pamphlet contained an introduction by Thomas Jefferson. In it, Jefferson not only praised Paine's views, he also criticized American political leaders who had strayed from "the revolutionary path." To John Quincy, this statement represented a direct attack on his father, who was now Vice-President of the United States. The elder Adams was widely—although incorrectly—regarded as being unsympathetic to democracy and in favor of a monarchy. That was too much!

Furious, John Quincy sat down and wrote a series of 11 essays criticizing Jefferson and arguing that the American constitution was superior to the doctrines of the French Revolution. The essays also advanced a political theory that John Quincy was to support all his life. *The Rights of Man* asserted that laws should reflect "the will of the majority." John Quincy disagreed. He felt this would lead to government by mob rule. The only way to maintain human rights, he argued, was to have a government based on a constitution that protected the rights of the minority even when those rights were contrary to what the majority believed in or wanted.

John Quincy's essays, published over the pen name of Publicola, attracted considerable attention both at home and abroad. In addition to appearing in a Boston newspaper, they were reprinted in London, Edinburgh (the capital of Scotland), and Dublin (the capital of Ireland). They were also translated into Dutch and French.

The attention greatly pleased John Quincy. So much so, in fact, that over the next three years he wrote four more series of political essays. One of the ideas he presented was the importance of staying out of European wars. The United States, John Quincy observed, had only a small army and an even smaller navy. As an infant nation, it had not yet had time to develop its natural resources or to build up its wealth. Under those circumstances, argued John Quincy, it was foolhardy to become involved overseas. The only result would be to risk the loss of America's hard-won independence.

A Presidential Honor

Among the people who read and admired John Quincy's essays was President George Washington. The young lawyer was eloquently expressing many of the President's own beliefs—especially the belief that the United States should avoid "entangling alliances" with foreign nations. So on May 29, 1794, Washington nominated John Quincy to the post of American ambassador to the Netherlands. The Senate approved the appointment unanimously the following day.

John and Abigail Adams were overjoyed. At last their son was beginning to assume the role for which he was destined! The Vice-President rushed off two long letters to his son full of advice. He told John Quincy to become familiar with all details of international law and of the various boundary disputes in which the United States was involved. He warned his son to beware of the English ambassador. Abigail's letter was equally full of advice, although of a different sort. John Quincy was reminded not to appear in public with his jacket wrinkled or his shirt soiled, and always to keep his fingernails free of dirt. He was also urged to stop being "something of a sourpuss." After all, as ambassador he was supposed to charm people, not drive them away.

John Quincy himself had mixed feelings. On the one hand, his law practice was now flourishing, and acccepting a ministerial post would mean taking a substantial reduction in pay. On the other hand, he would be on the international stage—and who knew what that might lead to? So, after several weeks of insomnia and what he called "a swimming in the head," John Quincy Adams, 27 years old, set sail on his third voyage to Europe.

Chapter 3

Diplomacy and Politics

J ohn Quincy Adams began his ambassadorial duties in the Netherlands on October 31, 1794. Almost immediately he found himself in a diplomatic dilemma.

England and France were once again at war. The Dutch ruler had sided with England and allowed a British army to be stationed in the Netherlands. The Dutch people were furious. Most of them were sympathetic with the French Revolution and supported France in the war. Then a French army invaded the Netherlands to counter the British threat. It won battle after battle. Alarmed at the rapid advance of the French, the Dutch ruler decided it was time to flee. He jumped into a fishing boat and headed across the English Channel to safety in England. The Dutch people promptly proclaimed themselves a republic.

Most of the foreign diplomats in the Netherlands left at the same time as the Dutch ruler. John Quincy decided to remain; not only that, on his own authority he recognized the new republic on behalf of the United States. The Dutch people had pressured their government to recognize the United States when it declared its independence, and John Quincy felt that turnabout was fair play.

Despite this promising start, John Quincy felt that there was not enough for him to do in the Netherlands. He handled some American loans to Dutch bankers. He also attended dinners with French generals, where he learned one of the secrets of their military success: an army fights more effectively if its officers are in the front lines rather than miles to the rear.

Beyond that, however, John Quincy thought his time in the Netherlands was wasted. "An American Minister at the Hague [then the capital of the Netherlands] is one of the most useless beings in creation," he complained in a letter to his father. He was little more than a reporter, John Quincy went on, and it was disgraceful for him to be "receiving the pay of a nation for the purpose of penetrating the contents of a newspaper."

John Adams held a different opinion. He pointed out that President Washington was highly pleased with "the clear, comprehensive and masterly accounts" of events in Europe that John Quincy was sending home. "Go on, my dear son," wrote John Adams encouragingly. "Continue to deserve well of your father, but especially of our country."

A MISSION TO ENGLAND

The following summer John Quincy was dispatched to London on a special assignment. While France was winning the war on the continent of Europe, England was using its powerful navy to choke off neutral shipping bound for France. British warships seized hundreds of American merchant vessels on the high seas. Often the British took over not only a ship's cargo but also part of its crew. They claimed the men were British seamen who had deserted His Majesty's Navy.

Sometimes they were right, for discipline in the British Navy was very harsh. Sailors were put in irons or flogged almost to death for such minor offenses as getting drunk. More often, however, the British were wrong, and the sailors they seized were actually American citizens. This policy of kidnapping men and forcing them to serve in the Royal Navy was known as impressment. Needless to say, it infuriated the Americans.

However, neither the United States nor England wanted to go to war over the matter. So the two nations signed a treaty dealing with freedom of the seas and the rights of neutrals. Unfortunately, the treaty did not mention impressment specifically. John Quincy's assignment in London was to try to change this.

Flattery and Insults

The British opened negotiations by flattering John Quincy outrageously, but he stuck to his position. Next, they tried to convince him that because he disapproved of the French Revolution, he should support England in its war against France. That approach did not work either. Then they tried to wear John Quincy down by shuttling him from one official to another. Finally, they insulted him by announcing that he was leaving London even before he had decided to go.

John Quincy felt he had failed. As he wrote to his father: "I have been accustomed all my life to plain dealing and candor, and am not sufficiently versed in the arts of political swindling to be prepared for negotiating with a European Minister of State."

John Quincy was being too hard on himself. Even though he did not obtain an agreement, he had not been taken in by flattery or cowed by insults. He had done the very best he could under the circumstances. It was a course of action he would follow all through his diplomatic and political career.

"Old Enough to Get Married"

Although John Quincy did not succeed in his diplomatic assignment in London, he *was* successful in another area. The American consul in London, Joshua Johnson, had seven daughters, three of whom were of marriageable age. During the winter of 1795, John Quincy courted the oldest daughter, Nancy. The following winter, however, he shifted his attentions to her sister Louisa, a quiet, gentle girl with delicate features and round black eyes. Like John Quincy, Louisa had loved and lost. And also like John Quincy, she was ready to settle for a suitable marriage based on respect.

After about a year, John Quincy proposed, Louisa accepted, and once again Abigail Adams put her foot down. As before, she argued economics. Although John Quincy was now financially independent, he did not own any property. Moreover, Mrs. Adams asserted, marrying a woman whose mother was English, not American, was bound to cause political controversy at home.

Abigail Adams was right. A Republican (Jeffersonian) newspaper, the *Independent Chronicle* of Boston, observed that "Young John Adams' negotiations have terminated in a marriage treaty with an English lady. . . . It is a happy circumstance that he has made no other [treaty on behalf of America]." At the same time, the engagement was defended by a Federalist newspaper, the *Columbian Centinel*, which declared that Louisa, even though raised in England, was an American because her father was an American. And in any event, John Quincy was representing the United States in Europe very ably indeed.

John Quincy ignored the political controversy. He did, however, write a bitter, self-pitying letter to his mother. He told her to stop meddling in his love affairs and accused her of having turned him from "a joyous youth into a cold and unsociable man" by breaking up his earlier relationship with Mary Frazier. Besides, at the age of 28 he was "old enough to get married." Taken aback, Abigail Adams withdrew her opposition, and John Quincy and Louisa were married in London on July 26, 1797.

MINISTER TO PRUSSIA

Soon after his marriage, John Quincy—having served three years as American ambassador to the Netherlands—was assigned a new diplomatic post. He was named America's first minister to Prussia. The appointment was made by his father, John Adams, who had succeeded George Washington as President of the United States.

The journey to John Quincy's new assignment proved to be a test of endurance. The first part of the trip, by ship from London to Hamburg, went well enough. But the second part, by land from Hamburg to Berlin, was another matter. The coach in which John and Louisa were traveling crawled over the muddy German roads at an average speed of half a mile an hour. The inns at which they stayed had bedbugs, and it sleeted most of the time.

At last, after some six weeks in transit, the couple arrived at the gate of Berlin. John Quincy presented his diplomatic credentials to the lieutenant in charge. The officer refused to let them in because he had never heard of the United States of America! John Quincy's temper was ready to explode. Fortunately, a private on duty *had* heard of the United States and managed to convince the lieutenant that the country really did exist. Minister and Mrs. Adams were permitted to enter Berlin.

An Able Diplomat

John Quincy spent four years in Berlin, from 1797 to 1801. During that time, he successfully negotiated a trade agreement between the United States and Prussia, but was unable to arrange for an American purchase of arms. He reluctantly wore formal court dress and attended the required official functions—balls, card parties, and reviews of the troops. But he much preferred to travel about the country, improving his German and learning as much as possible about politics and the people. As before, he drafted long, informative reports that he sent to his father. He also spent as much of his spare time as he could reading history books and writing poems and essays.

In 1800 President John Adams was defeated for reelection by Vice-President Thomas Jefferson. It was a strongly partisan election, and the bitterness between the Federalists (who supported Adams) and the Republicans (who supported Jefferson) was great. Accordingly, President Adams, unwilling to give Jefferson the satisfaction of doing so, recalled his son from his ministerial post. Jefferson, however, had no intention of removing John Quincy, whom he regarded as one of the country's ablest diplomats. But "the deed was done." So in September 1801, John Quincy, Louisa, and their baby son, George Washington Adams, returned to the United States, where John Quincy reluctantly resumed the practice of law.

A CHANGED NATION

During the seven years that John Quincy had been in Europe, the United States had changed considerably. For one thing, it looked different. As John Quincy wrote in his diary, "I find everywhere the marks of peace within our walls, and prosperity within our palaces – for palaces they may truly be called, those splendid and costly mansions which since my departure seem to have shot up from the earth by enchantment." What had happened was that England and France were temporarily at peace, and New England's maritime trade was flourishing as never before. Hundreds of American sailing vessels crowded the sea lanes, carrying goods across the Atlantic and bringing increased wealth to the nation's merchants and manufacturers.

There were political changes as well. Under the influence of Secretary of the Treasury Alexander Hamilton, the federal government had established control over the nation's economy. The United States now had a central banking system. It also had a national tariff, or tax on imported goods. It even had a national tax: an excise, or sales, tax on whiskey.

The Federalists and the Republicans

As a result of Hamilton's fiscal policies, the federal government was able to support itself without state funds. Business people approved, and they formed the core of the Federalist Party. In general, Federalists distrusted the French Revolution and tended to put property rights above individual rights. They favored a broad interpretation of the U.S. Constitution, arguing that the federal government could take whatever steps were needed to exercise its powers, even if those steps were not specifically mentioned in the Constitution. John Quincy, like his father, was a Federalist. So were most people in New England.

Elsewhere in the country, though, Americans favored the Republican Party, headed by Thomas Jefferson. In fact, in addition to the presidency, the Republicans now controlled both houses of Congress, as well as 13 of the 16 state legislatures. As John Quincy observed, "The power of the administration rests upon a stronger majority of the people throughout the Union than the former administrations ever possessed." Most Republicans preferred France to England, tended to value individual rights more than property rights, and favored a strict interpretation of the U.S. Constitution.

ENTERING POLITICS

Although John Quincy had resumed his law practice in Boston, his heart was still in public life. He found law boring, and he greatly missed the excitement of the diplomatic arena. Besides, he wanted to carry on the Adams tradition of public service.

John Quincy's first opportunity to enter politics came in 1802, when he was chosen by the Federalist Party to run for the Massachusetts State Senate. He won election easily. But within 48 hours after taking his seat, he managed to antagonize party leaders. He supported a bill to give Republicans a share of the seats on the governor's council. A short time later, he voted against the establishment of a new bank in Boston supported by party leaders. His reason was that stock in the bank was to be sold only to "gentlemen of respectable character." John Quincy felt that since the stock would be issued publicly rather than privately, it should be available to everyone who could afford it.

Federalist leaders grumbled. "Young Adams appears to be unmanageable," they muttered. "This man is not our friend, but against us." And they were right, for John Quincy did not like party dictation. "A politician in this country must be the man of a party," he wrote in his diary. *"I would [rather] be the man of my whole country."*

Despite John Quincy's maverick behavior, the Federalist-controlled state legislature elected him a United States senator in 1803. (U.S. senators were not chosen by popular vote until 1913.) The Adams name carried a great deal of weight in Massachusetts. The legislators apparently hoped that John Quincy Adams, having proven his independence in the Massachusetts Senate, would turn into a loyal party member in Congress. They were mistaken.

Life in Washington

In 1803 Washington, D.C., was little more than a rough village. Several years earlier, a French architect named Pierre L'Enfant had drawn up a grand design for the city, with broad squares and sweeping avenues. But almost none of the design had yet been implemented. There was just one street, Pennsylvania Avenue. It stretched for 1¾ miles between the Capitol and the President's house, then known as the Presidential Castle. The street was unpaved, muddy in winter and dusty in summer. Herds of cows, geese, and swine wandered about loose. A few frame boardinghouses and a ragged collection of stables, shops, taverns, and poorly designed government buildings were scattered along either side of the street. The areas that had been set aside by L'Enfant for parks were filled with weeds. There was not a single church in town. The city was commonly described as a "wilderness city" and as a "capital of miserable huts."

Fortunately, Adams and his family did not have to live in Washington. Instead, he, Louisa, and their two sons moved in with Louisa's sister Nancy. She, too, had married an American, a rich tobacco speculator named Walter Hellen who owned a large house in the nearby village of Georgetown.

John Quincy soon settled into a routine. He would rise between five and six o'clock in the morning and spend three hours reading such "works of instruction" as the Bible, the Latin classics, and Adam Smith's *Wealth of Nations*. After breakfast, he would walk the 2½ miles to the Capitol, where he would work on one of the numerous committees to which he had been assigned. The Senate session began at noon. Afterwards, Adams would walk back to Georgetown. Sometimes he ate dinner at home; at other times he attended government functions. Despite his political differences with President Jefferson, he often dined at the Presidential Castle, where the two men held lively discussions over nuts and Madeira wine.

THE LOUISIANA PURCHASE

It did not take long for Adams to show his independent streak. He had barely been sworn in as senator when he broke party ranks over the issue of the Louisiana Purchase.

In 1800 France had signed a secret treaty with Spain under which it reacquired all the land in the western part of the Mississippi Valley that it had lost in 1763. By 1803, however, France was once again at war with England and badly in need of money. So the French ruler, Napoleon Bonaparte, offered to sell the United States some 828,000 square miles of land between the Mississippi River and the Rocky Mountains. The price was $15 million in gold, or about three cents an acre.

The Louisiana Purchase was the greatest real estate deal in history. It not only doubled America's area, it also eliminated a base for a foreign empire and gave the United States control over the Mississippi River trade.

The only people who objected to the deal were New England Federalists. They feared that the new states that would be carved out of the Louisiana Territory would weaken the political power of their region in favor of the South and West. Moreover, the new states might be slave states, and slavery had by this time been abolished in New England.

Adams had arrived in Washington a few hours too late to vote on the purchase itself, but he soon made his position clear. First he endorsed the purchase publicly, then he voted in favor of issuing bonds to pay for the purchase. Finally, to the horror of other Federalist senators, he attended a Republican banquet celebrating the purchase.

Country First

Adams' attitude was country first, state and party second. As he wrote in his diary: "Each Senator is a representation not of a single State, but of the whole Union." John Quincy also strongly supported what became known later as "Manifest Destiny." This was the belief that America was destined to stretch from the Atlantic Ocean to the Pacific Ocean. The taking, not just of Louisiana but of the entire North American continent by the United States, was "as much a law of nature . . . as that the Mississippi should flow to the sea."

To Massachusetts Federalists, however, John Quincy's actions smacked of treason to his party and his region. A Boston banker angrily accused him of being "a kite without a tail," who was more concerned with ambition than with principle. And a Worcester newspaper predicted that "The Hon. John Quincy Adams will certainly be denounced and [expelled] by his party."

A CLASH AT SEA

Adams once again angered Federalist Party leaders and his New England neighbors when he sided with President Jefferson to prohibit Americans from trading overseas. The war between England and France had turned into a stalemate, with each side trying to strangle the other by a blockade. This included seizing American merchant ships and their cargoes. To add insult to injury, the British were still impressing American sailors.

The issue came to a head in 1807. The captain of the British warship *Leopard* demanded that a crew be allowed to board the American frigate *Chesapeake* to search for deserters. The captain of the *Chesapeake* refused. The *Leopard* then fired on the unprepared *Chesapeake*, killing three Americans and wounding 18. The *Chesapeake* had no choice but to surrender and give up four men, two of them Americans. It then limped back to port. This was the first time the British had seized an American military vessel. To make matters worse, the incident took place within sight of Norfolk, Virginia.

When news of the *Leopard-Chesapeake* affair reached Boston, Adams was teaching a course in rhetoric at Harvard.

He immediately called on local Federalist leaders to stage a mass protest rally. The Federalists hesitated. In spite of the shipping losses the English and French blockades caused, foreign trade was booming, and New England shipbuilders and merchants were growing rich. Why upset the status quo (the existing state of affairs)? So the rally was staged instead by the Republicans — and Adams not only attended but also helped draft the protest resolutions.

A few months later, President Jefferson asked Congress to embargo, or prohibit, American foreign trade. He hoped the action would force England and France to respect the right of neutral America to freedom of the seas. Senator Adams was the only Federalist in Congress to support Jefferson.

Removal from Office

Unfortunately, matters did not work out as the President had hoped. The embargo hurt neither England nor France. Instead, its main burden fell on the United States, especially on New England. American exports dropped 80 percent in one year, farm prices tumbled, shipyards stood idle, grass began to grow on the docks, and thousands of people were thrown out of work. Things became so bad, in fact, that some New Englanders began talking about seceding from (leaving) the Union. An example of popular opinion at the time was the following ballad, which originated in Massachusetts:

> Our ships all in motion once whitened the ocean,
>   They sailed and returned with a cargo;
> Now doomed to decay, they have fallen a prey
>   To Jefferson — worms — and Embargo.

Through it all, Adams kept urging the United States to

stand firm and not give in to British demands. To do so, he argued, would cost America its hard-won independence. Federalist newspapers responded by calling him such names as "apostate," "popularity seeker," "turncoat," and "party scavenger." But the senator would not budge. "Private interests must not be put in opposition to public good," he stated.

The result was that the Federalists dumped Adams from office. His term as U.S. senator was due to expire at the end of 1808. However, instead of waiting until then, the Federalist-controlled legislature in Massachusetts met six months ahead of schedule and chose a wealthy merchant as John Quincy's successor. Stung by the action, Adams promptly resigned from the Senate and returned to Boston to resume the practice of law once again.

Chapter 4

Mr. Madison's War, Mr. Adams' Peace

Fortunately for John Quincy's state of mind, his renewed legal career lasted only a few months. Although Jefferson's embargo failed, another Republican, James Madison, succeeded him as President. By this time, the Republicans considered Adams as one of their own, even though he was not an official party member. So in March 1809, Madison nominated Adams as America's first ambassador to Russia, and the Senate approved the choice three months later.

John Quincy welcomed the assignment in his usual restrained manner. "I could see no sufficient reason for refusing the nomination," he wrote in his diary. Accompanied by Louisa and two-year-old Charles Francis, the youngest of their three sons, he set out for St. Petersburg, where he had begun his diplomatic career 28 years before. The two older boys stayed behind with relatives in Massachusetts.

THE COURT OF ST. PETERSBURG

In those years, the Russian court was the most lavish in Europe. Noblemen dined on plates of solid gold. Women sparkled with diamonds and wore a different gown to every ball.

There were sleighing parties during the day and receptions, masquerades, and dinner parties at night. The festivities often lasted until the middle of the following morning. John Quincy thoroughly disapproved of the "irregularity" and "dissipation" of court life. He much preferred such solitary pleasures as reading, translating, and visiting local libraries and museums.

John Quincy also found himself socially limited by the modest salary of $9,000 the federal government paid him. Out of this, he had to rent a house and feed and support a steward, a cook, two scullions (kitchen helpers), a porter, two footmen, a janitor, a coachman, a valet, a personal maid, a house maid, and a laundry maid, to say nothing of their families. "The firewood is, luckily, included as part of my rent." Other diplomats and special-interest seekers offered him loans and outright gifts, but Adams turned them all down. He did not want to compromise his independence in any way. The only solution was to live frugally and entertain as seldom as possible.

An Admirable Ambassador

Adams was now 42 years old. His face was etched with lines. His harsh voice, like that of his father, grated on people's ears, and he was very blunt in what he said. Yet despite his lack of social graces, he made an admirable ambassador. He spoke French, German, and Dutch fluently and soon learned Russian as well. He had a quick, analytical mind as well as the ability to persuade others of his point of view. He certainly knew a great deal more about the nations of Europe – their resources, interests, and relationships – than anyone else in the diplomatic corps.

Adams was further helped in his work by his friendship with the Russian czar, Alexander I. Both men enjoyed walking, and they often found themselves strolling together through the streets of St. Petersburg, chatting in French. One day the czar told Adams that he sometimes did not recognize the American ambassador outside of court because he looked so different without his wig. Since the czar did not seem to object to his natural appearance, Adams, who hated wigs anyway and only wore them because it was the custom at court, never put on a wig again.

Diplomatic Difficulties

Among the issues John Quincy and Alexander I discussed was the ongoing war between France and England. Adams was upset because some 40 American merchant ships attempting to run France's blockade of Europe had been seized by Denmark as prizes of war. Denmark argued that it had no choice. How could it resist Napoleon's orders? Ambassador Adams convinced the czar to offer military protection to Denmark if it would release the American vessels, and Denmark agreed.

Adams' diplomatic success, however, had unforeseen results. Not only did more American ships brave Europe's northern waters, but British vessels disguised themselves as American and did the same. The furious French emperor thereupon demanded that the czar join his blockade and close Russia's ports to all ships flying the American flag. But because Russia was heavily dependent on its commercial trade with the United States, Alexander rejected Napoleon's demand—and relations between France and Russia became worse.

"War Hawks"

In the meantime, relations between England and the United States were also worsening. The Royal Navy was still preying on American ships and impressing American sailors. In addition, the year 1810 had seen the election to Congress of a large number of "war hawks." They came mostly from the newer western states, and they were a different breed from the representatives of New England and other states along the Atlantic seaboard.

Unlike their counterparts in the eastern states, who had to own property to vote, all white men in the western states could vote. As a result, the representatives they elected were often less educated than eastern congressmen. Since they came from frontier areas, they tended to be tough, outspoken, and impatient. They were also young, in their early thirties. Having been born after the United States became independent, they were extremely nationalistic. They did not resent England because it was hurting America's foreign trade. Rather, they resented England because they felt its actions were an insult to their country. And like Adams, the "war hawks" were strong believers in Manifest Destiny. As one congressman put it, "The Author of Nature has marked out our limits in the South, by the Gulf of Mexico, and on the North by the regions of eternal frost." In other words, the "war hawks" wanted to conquer Canada, England's only remaining colony in North America.

A YEAR OF WAR

The year 1812 turned out to be a fateful one for both the United States and Russia. On June 18 President Madison—unable to resist the "war hawks" any longer—reluctantly asked Congress to declare war against England. And on June 24 Napoleon invaded Russia.

Both the Americans and the French soon suffered resounding defeats. The United States had only a small, poorly trained army and a navy of 16 ships. Its first "drive to the north" resulted in the loss of Detroit and the capture of the entire American force. Its second and third expeditions into Canada were equally unsuccessful.

At the same time, the French succumbed to what Adams called "General Famine and General Frost." By the time Napoleon's soldiers reached Moscow, they were short of supplies, and one of the bitterest Russian winters in history was underway. When Moscow burned down, their last source of food and shelter was destroyed. Napoleon was forced to turn around and head back to France.

Adams commented gloomily on both the American and the French defeats in a letter to his parents. He could scarcely hold a pen in his hands because it was so cold in St. Petersburg. The temperature had been below zero for 17 successive days, and even double windows and heated stoves made little difference. Perhaps, Adams observed, it was "contrary to the course of nature for men of the South to invade the regions of the North. Napoleon should have thought of that. So should the [American] visitors of . . . Canada."

Steps Toward Peace

John Quincy was much more optimistic in another letter he wrote that winter, one to Secretary of State James Monroe. The Russian government had been dismayed by the outbreak of the Anglo-American war. It was afraid the United States would ally itself with France because France was fighting England. So the czar informed Adams that he was prepared to do whatever he could to bring about peace between England and the United States.

John Quincy was delighted. He felt the war was hurting the United States and helping no one except Napoleon, whom he considered a tyrant. So instead of writing to Washington for instructions, Adams took it on himself to accept the Russian offer. Then he informed Monroe about what he had done.

Fortunately for Adams' diplomatic career, both Monroe and Madison approved, and the President immediately sent special envoys to join Adams in St. Petersburg. Nevertheless, peace negotiations did not actually get under way for another 18 months. First, it took the envoys six months to reach Russia. Then England rejected the idea of using a third party, and it took Czar Alexander another six months to convince the British to negotiate directly with their former colony. Next, the two sides wrangled over where the negotiations were to take place. But at last, in August 1814, five Americans and three Englishmen sat down together in the city of Ghent, in Belgium.

The Treaty of Ghent

Both sides wanted peace. For England, the conflict with America was draining its manpower and its pocketbook. For the United States, its military record—except for a few battles in the Great Lakes region—was a disaster. The Americans could not even prevent the British from entering Washington and setting it on fire. Furthermore, many New Englanders were so unhappy over the course of the war and the damage to their overseas trade that they were once again threatening to secede. So the real issue at Ghent was the terms on which peace could be arranged.

The Star-Spangled Banner

The British burning of Washington, D.C., and their subsequent attack on Baltimore, Maryland, led to the writing of the words to America's national anthem, ''The Star-Spangled Banner.'' The author was a Washington lawyer: Francis Scott Key.

When the British left Washington for Baltimore, they took with them as prisoner a friend of Key's named William Beanes. Key asked President Madison if he might negotiate with the British for Beanes' release, and the President gave his permission. So Key and a companion, John S. Skinner, went aboard one of the British warships in Chesapeake Bay to discuss the matter. The British agreed to Beanes' relase. However, they were just getting ready to bombard Fort McHenry, which stood at the entrance to Baltimore Harbor. Since the British did not want Key to warn the Americans on shore about the impending attack, they put him, Skinner, and Beanes in a small prisoner-exchange boat at the rear of their fleet.

The bombardment began early Tuesday morning, September 13, 1814. All that day, British naval guns rained destruction on the fort. The shelling continued through the night. Key could not sleep. He paced the deck, wondering whether Fort McHenry would be able to withstand the heavy assault. As the sun rose, he strained his eyes in the fort's direction, trying to see through the smoke and haze. Suddenly, the smoke and haze lifted for a moment—and Key saw the American flag still waving in the air. Thrilled and delighted, he pulled some paper from his pocket and began to write.

Later that day, September 14, Key and his friends were released. The next day, Key's poem was printed on handbills. Soon everyone in Baltimore had a copy. Several days later, an actor named Ferdinand Durang— using the tune of an English drinking song— sang Key's verses in public.

"The Star-Spangled Banner" became popular immediately, not just in Baltimore but throughout the nation. However, it was not officially adopted as the country's national anthem for some time. For one thing, there was competition from "Hail Columbia," written by Joseph Hopkinson. For another thing, some people objected to the strongly anti-British third verse, which they considered inappropriate for a national anthem:

> And where is that band who so
>   vauntingly swore
> That the havoc of war and the battle's
>   confusion
> A home and a country should leave us
>   no more?
> Their blood has washed out their foul
>   footstep's pollution.
> No refuge could save the hireling and
>   slave
> From the terror of flight or the gloom of
>   the grave,

> And the star-spangled banner in triumph
> doth wave
> O'er the land of the free and the home of
> the brave.
>
> By 1850, however, "The Star-Spangled
> Banner" was found in most school songbooks
> in the United States. By the 1890s, both the
> U.S. Army and the U.S. Navy were playing it
> at all ceremonial events. Finally, in 1931, the
> song was officially approved by Congress as
> the national anthem.
>
> The flag that waved over Fort McHenry
> contained 15 stripes and 15 stars. In 1818,
> Congress set the number of stripes at 13 for
> the 13 original states. Each time a new state
> joined the Union, Congress said, another star
> was to be added. It was not until 1887 that
> all U.S. Army units were required to carry the
> Stars and Stripes. And it was not until 1912
> that the flag's design became the only official
> one allowed.

As head of the American delegation, Adams naturally took a serious view of his responsibilities. "The welfare of my family and country, with the interests of humanity, are staked upon the event." However, he also took a serious view of how the other four American peace commissioners should behave.

Adams himself kept up his usual routine of rising at dawn to read the Bible, dining at one, visiting bookshops and museums in his spare time, and going to bed at nine. The four other commissioners behaved differently. They went to coffeehouses and played billiards. "They sit after dinner and drink bad wine and smoke cigars, which neither suits my habits nor my health." (John Quincy had given up both drinking and smoking.) Once, Adams complained, he actually heard an all-night card party breaking up in the room of commissioner Henry Clay just as he himself was getting up! Fortunately, another commissioner, Albert Gallatin, was able to keep Adams from losing his temper and voicing his disapproval.

In spite of their personal differences, the American commissioners worked well as a diplomatic team. Under Adams' leadership, they slowly beat back one British demand after another. No, they would not agree to the establishment of an Indian nation around the shores of Lake Michigan. No, they would not give the British control of the Great Lakes and the right to sail the Mississippi. And yes, American fishermen should be allowed to continue fishing off the eastern coast of Canada.

As for the issues of freedom of the seas and impressment—two of the main causes of the War of 1812— nothing at all was said. The reason was that by this time both issues had disappeared. Even before war broke out, England had changed its policy and decided not to seize any more American merchant ships. But the news did not reach Washington until after war was declared. Also, Napoleon had finally been defeated. So England no longer needed to impress large numbers of sailors for its navy.

At last, after five months of negotiations, the Treaty of Ghent was signed on Christmas Eve, 1814. It was really an armistice (a truce) rather than a treaty, for it left everything the way it had been before the war. Differences over the Canadian-American boundary and other disputes were to be

The heads of the American and British delegations at Ghent shake hands to celebrate the signing of the peace treaty. The simple clothes of Adams and the other Americans contrast with the fancy uniforms trimmed in gold braid worn by the British. (National Museum of Art, Smithsonian Institution, Gift of the Sulgrave Institution of the United States and Great Britain.)

settled later by a joint commission. Nevertheless, for a young nation that had almost lost the war and was in no position to drive a hard bargain, the treaty was a great achievement. As Adams wrote Louisa: "We have obtained nothing but peace. . . . But our honor remains unsullied; our territory remains entire."

Actually, the United States obtained more than peace. It also obtained the admiration and respect of Europe for having once again stood up to its former ruler.

For the next two weeks, both sides celebrated the signing of the treaty. A solemn service was held in the cathedral of Ghent, and there were banquets, balls, and concerts. Bands alternated between playing "Hail Columbia" and "God Save the King." John Quincy acknowledged his pleasure: "I left this place with such recollections as I never carried from any other spot in Europe."

AMBASSADOR TO ENGLAND

A few months later, as a reward for negotiating the Treaty of Ghent, Adams was appointed ambassador to England. He was very pleased, for the London post was the most important one in America's diplomatic service. Louisa was equally pleased. She had always considered Russia "a horrid place" and looked forward to the warmer (even if rainier) climate of England. In addition, Adams agreed to have their two oldest sons rejoin the family.

So the five Adamses settled down in a small country house about a two-hour carriage ride outside of London. There, John Quincy went hiking with his sons, taught them how to shoot a pistol, and at night peered with them through a telescope, pointing out the various constellations. He also found time to write poetry. As in Russia, he spent most of his evenings attending social functions. And as before, he found it very difficult to entertain on his salary. If this kept up, he warned Secretary of State Monroe, the only people who could become ambassadors would be "men of large fortune willing to spend it liberally."

An Accessible Ambassador

John Quincy tried to be accessible to every American who knocked on the embassy door. And hundreds did. There were sailors who had been impressed by the British and needed help in returning home. There were wealthy young men traveling to Europe to finish their education. There were inventors in search of financial support, and people anxious to trace their family lineage. Some of their demands were such that John Quincy once complained bitterly about "the multitudes of people, who . . . apply for what cannot be granted, and often for what is improper, are so importunate [annoyingly urgent], . . . so unreasonable, sometimes so insolent and consume so much time."

At the same time, Adams had to carry on an extensive correspondence—in longhand—with "the ministers, agents or consuls of the United States in Russia, Sweden, Holland, France, Spain, Italy, the Barbary Coast and Brazil, with the commanders of the American squadron in the Mediterranean, and particularly with the American consuls in the ports of Great Britain, Ireland, Gibraltar and Malta; and with the bankers and navy agents of the United States in the Mediterranean, at London, and at Amsterdam."

On the diplomatic front, Adams succeeded in negotiating a trade treaty between the United States and England. The two nations agreed not to levy discriminatory taxes on the goods they bought and sold to each other. In addition, American merchant ships were allowed to trade with the British East Indies.

Adams also suggested that the Great Lakes boundary between Canada and the United States be left unguarded. Neither nation would maintain a costly fleet of warships on the lakes. Instead, each country would operate only those vessels needed to collect customs duties on goods that were shipped across the Great Lakes. Adams' suggestion was eventually adopted in 1817.

A NEW POST

All this time, John Quincy's father kept writing his son and urging him to come home. John Adams needed someone to help him edit his memoirs. He wanted to see his grandsons again. John Quincy had been out of the United States for eight years now, and John Adams argued that further absence would make an elective public career impossible. "You are now approaching fifty years of age. In my opinion, you must return to your country, or renounce it forever."

John Quincy agreed with his father that if he wanted an elective public career, he had to return home. But how could he earn a living? He did not want to be an editor. And he disliked law so much that he had turned down an appointment to the United States Supreme Court!

Then, in 1816, the difficulty was resolved. James Monroe was elected President to succeed James Madison. And the President-elect offered John Quincy the post of secretary of state.

Chapter 5

Secretary of State

Becoming secretary of state was a real plum for John Quincy. Not only was it the highest diplomatic post in the nation, but since the turn of the century it had served as a stepping-stone to the presidency. Jefferson, Madison, and Monroe had all been secretaries of state before they were elected chief executive. The post was an excellent training ground. As the senior Cabinet member, the secretary of state could expect to take part in all major presidential decisions and learn firsthand what was involved in administering the government and leading the people.

Adams was overjoyed at the appointment. He had never forgotten his mother's words about "family destiny" when, almost 40 years before, she had persuaded John Quincy to accompany his father on his second trip to Europe. When John Adams was elected President, it seemed clear to John Quincy what "family destiny" meant. Ever since, he had secretly looked upon himself as a sort of "heir" who would one day become President just like his father.

The only matter that troubled Adams was why Monroe had chosen him. True, he was unquestionably the most knowledgeable American in the field of foreign affairs. But he had, after all, been out of the country for many years. As it happens, that was one of the main reasons he *was* chosen. He had not taken part in the Federalist vs. Republican politicking that had gone on during the War of 1812. Also, he was a northerner, and Monroe, a southerner from Virginia, wanted both regions to be properly represented in the executive branch of the federal government.

RUNNING THE STATE DEPARTMENT

Although Washington was small and crude compared to St. Petersburg and London, Adams did not mind. He did not even complain about all the social functions he had to attend. He was determined to do everything he could to make the United States strong, secure, and respected.

Adams began by straightening out the State Department. When he arrived, he found his desk covered with letters and dispatches, unorganized and seemingly unread. Worse, the terms of a treaty with Sweden had apparently been lost somewhere. Adams immediately set up a filing system and an index for all diplomatic letters and documents. He also had Louisa make copies of his correspondence for his private letter books.

In addition, Adams undertook a number of administrative tasks. He supervised the national census. He managed the printing and distribution of the laws passed by Congress. He even researched and wrote a report on weights and measures in which he urged the United States to adopt the metric system, which France had recently developed. He hoped this would set an example for the rest of the world.

Adams also dealt with the question of protocol (code of behavior for diplomats). Like all capitals, Washington was a social city, and the question regarding whose wife should

Louisa Catherine Adams did not care for the social life of Washington, even though she was an excellent hostess. This portrait of her was painted about 1824. (National Museum of American Art, Smithsonian Institution, Adams-Clement Collection, Gift of Mary Louisa Adams Clement in memory of her mother, Louisa Catherine Adams Clement.)

make the first social call was a serious matter that was even discussed in the Cabinet. Mrs. Madison had called on everyone. "Mrs. Monroe," Adams noted in his diary, "neither pays nor returns any visits." Louisa decided that she would call on the wives of foreign ambassadors only after they called on her. Although the wives of the ambassadors complained bitterly to Mrs. Monroe, Louisa stood her ground – and John Quincy agreed. He felt it was the only course of behavior that showed proper respect for the American government.

Facing the Canadian Border Dispute

On the diplomatic front, Adams was faced with the task of settling the Anglo-American disagreements that had not been resolved by the Treaty of Ghent. The major dispute was the location of America's northern border.

The easternmost part of the boundary, between Canada and Maine, remained unsettled until 1842. However, after a series of discussions, the boundary between the Louisiana Purchase and Canada was fixed at the 49th parallel as far west as the Rocky Mountains. West of the Rockies, a joint British-American commission was to administer the Oregon Country – which both nations claimed – for a ten-year period. As Adams had suggested several years earlier, the Canadian-American boundary was to be a peaceful one, with each side maintaining only four small warships on the Great Lakes. Today, the border (extended to the Pacific Ocean) is the longest unguarded international boundary in the world.

GAINING FLORIDA

Adams next turned to securing the nation's southern and western borders. Here his main diplomatic opponent was Spain, and the major source of trouble was Florida.

In Adams' eyes, the United States could have no real territorial security as long as Florida belonged to Spain. If war broke out, Spanish troops were near enough to attack New Orleans and close the Mississippi River to American trade. Then, too, the Spanish had allowed Seminole Indians free rein to raid settlements across the frontier in Georgia. And for years the Seminoles had given refuge to black fugitive slaves from the United States. In any event, as a firm believer in Manifest Destiny, Adams considered Florida to be a natural continuation of American territory.

Andrew Jackson and the Seminole War

During the War of 1812, the British built a fort in Florida on the Apalachicola River. When the war ended, the British agent in charge turned the fort over to a fugitive slave from the United States named Garson. Garson invited other fugitive slaves in Florida to settle near the fort, and soon both banks of the river were lined with black settlements for a distance of 50 miles.

Georgia planters, alarmed that the settlements would encourage mass attempts at escape by their slaves, called for action. So in 1816 American troops invaded Florida and blew up the fort. Although most of its defenders were killed, the blacks in the nearby settlements escaped and took refuge with Seminole Indians farther east. The Georgia planters again called for action, and in 1817 a series of clashes between Georgia frontiersmen and Seminoles provided the excuse for a second American invasion of Florida.

The leader of the American forces was Andrew Jackson. Jackson had won a national reputation as a bold military campaigner during the War of 1812. Two weeks after the

A schoolmate of Andrew Jackson's described one of the future President's main qualities when he said, "I could throw him three times out of four but he would never stay throwed. *He was dead game even then, and never would give up."* (Library of Congress.)

signing of the Treaty of Ghent but before news of it crossed the Atlantic, he had defeated a British army at the Battle of New Orleans. In addition, Jackson—like Adams—was a fervent nationalist who believed Florida should be part of the United States.

Jackson's marching orders were limited. He was to invade Florida and attack the Seminole Indians along the border. However, if the Seminoles "should shelter under a Spanish post," Jackson was to notify the War Department before taking any further action.

Jackson immediately began collecting volunteers for the invasion. He also wrote a secret note to President Monroe, stating that if "the possession of the Floridas is desirable to the United States . . . in sixty days it will be accomplished."

In later years, Monroe claimed that he had simply passed the note along to Secretary of War John C. Calhoun. Jackson claimed that he had received an unofficial but definite go-ahead. In any event, on March 10, 1818, Jackson issued each of his soldiers a ration of meat and corn and crossed the border into Florida.

Crisis Over Florida

In the meantime, Adams was holding talks with the Spanish ambassador in Washington. At issue was the western boundary of the United States. Spain had never recognized the Louisiana Purchase and kept insisting that the border between the United States and Mexico should be the Mississippi River. Adams, of course, refused to even consider such a position. As far as he was concerned, America stretched to the Pacific Ocean. Neither side would give way.

Then, in June 1818, news of Jackson's actions in Florida

reached Washington. After burning several Seminole villages, Jackson had continued his advance and had captured the Spanish fort of St. Marks. He had also captured two British citizens, an elderly trader named Alexander Arbuthnot and a young soldier of fortune named Robert C. Armbrister, who had apparently been stirring up the Seminoles against the Americans. Jackson ordered them killed as a "necessary warning" against any further Indian agitation. Jackson had then captured the Spanish town of Pensacola and appointed one of his colonels as governor of Florida.

Immediately, a furor erupted in Washington. Congress may have wanted to acquire Florida, but it had not authorized taking it by force. Both the House and the Senate roundly condemned Jackson's behavior and called for an investigation. In addition, Spain sent a blistering note of protest. And in London, after learning of the execution of the two British subjects, members of Parliament called angrily for a declaration of war. The United States was still recovering from the War of 1812, and the last thing it needed was another conflict with England. What to do?

A Diplomatic Coup

President Monroe and his Cabinet met five times in six days to discuss the crisis. Almost everyone felt that Jackson had exceeded his orders and embarrassed the government, and that he should be fired forthwith. The only person who disagreed was Adams.

John Quincy realized that if the American government did not stand behind Jackson, its bargaining position with Spain would be seriously weakened. Then it would not be possible to obtain either Florida or territories along the Pacific.

So Adams went on the offensive. Instead of defending the United States, he attacked Spain. His main weapon was a letter he wrote to the American ambassador in Madrid, Spain, copies of which were sent to every foreign office in Europe. In the letter, Adams argued that Jackson's motives were "purest patriotism . . . acting in the first law of nature, self-defense." Spain was obviously too weak to control its own possessions. Otherwise, why had it allowed the Indians and their British sponsors to use Florida as a base of operations against the United States? This was a particularly effective argument because several of Spain's colonies in Latin America had recently revolted.

Adams did not stop there. He went on to criticize Great Britain in no uncertain terms. "From the period of our established independence to this day, *all* the Indian wars with which we have been afflicted have been distinctly traceable to the instigation of English traders or agents." Under the circumstances, Adams wrote, Jackson's punishment of Arbuthnot and Armbrister was completely justified. Furthermore, if Great Britain continued meddling in American affairs, the United States would have no choice but to respond actively.

The results of the letter were all that Adams could have hoped for, both at home and abroad. Congress abandoned its investigations into the Florida invasion. England, anxious to keep the United States as a market for its manufactured goods, decided that there was no point in going to war after all. And Spain, worried about its rebellious colonies in Latin America and seeing that it would get no help from England, decided that the best thing to do was to work out a territorial agreement with the United States.

In 1819 Secretary of State Adams and the Spanish ambassador signed the Transcontinental Treaty, also known as the Adams-Onís Treaty. In exchange for $5 million, the United States obtained Florida. In the West, it established the border between the United States and Mexico all the way to the Pacific Ocean. That night, John Quincy wrote in his diary that "It was perhaps the most important day of my life."

THE MONROE DOCTRINE

Four years later, in 1823, Adams followed up his diplomatic success with Spain with another coup. Most of Spain's colonies in Latin America had recently won their independence, and the United States became the first nation to recognize them. Almost immediately, however, France and Russia began rattling their swords and threatening to support "the supremacy of Spain over its revolted colonies." Great Britain, on the other hand, saw an opportunity to gain a vast new market for its manufactured goods. So it proposed to Adams that the two nations issue a joint declaration warning other European nations not to interfere in the Western Hemisphere. The declaration would be enforced by the Royal Navy, which controlled the Atlantic.

Adams liked the idea, but he mistrusted England. He was convinced the British would use a joint declaration to keep the United States from expanding farther into Spanish territory—and Adams' vision of Manifest Destiny included Cuba and the northern part of Mexico. Moreover, he did not like the idea of hiding behind the British fleet. "It would be more [honest] as well as more dignified to [openly declare] our principles . . . than to come in as a cock-boat [behind] the British man-of-war."

So Adams prepared a statement that President Monroe included in his State of the Union message to Congress. Known as the Monroe Doctrine, the statement combined a warning with a pledge. European nations were not to set up new colonies in the Western Hemisphere, nor were they to attack the newly independent Latin American republics. If they did, the United States would consider it "dangerous to our peace and safety." In return, the United States promised not to interfere with existing European colonies. It also promised to stay out of Europe's internal affairs.

This was a bold stand for a young nation to take. Yet the Monroe Doctrine—which could really be called the Monroe-Adams Doctrine— had clear advantages. It gained the support of the Royal Navy without a formal alliance with England. And it served notice on Europe that the United States was now first in the Western Hemisphere. No longer was it concerned only with its own safety and growth; it was also assuming certain responsibilities for Latin America. The Monroe Doctrine remained a cornerstone of America's foreign policy through the 19th and early 20th centuries.

Chapter 6

The Election of 1824

All during his tenure as secretary of state, Adams anticipated fulfilling his dream of becoming President. But as the election of 1824 drew near, it no longer seemed as certain as it had eight years earlier that he would be elected. The tradition of stepping up from the State Department to the White House was being challenged by changes within the United States.

The major change was the westward movement of the American people. A majority of the population now lived west of the Allegheny Mountains instead of along the eastern seaboard. Since western states had abolished property requirements for voting, political power there belonged to the "common people." And the "common people" did not regard men of family and education—such as John Quincy Adams—as heroes. They favored such individuals as Henry Clay of Kentucky and Andrew Jackson of Tennessee, who were like themselves. Also, they were suspicious of having an outgoing President more or less choose his successor. Besides, they wanted someone from their own region.

THE POLITICAL CLIMATE

Adams' chances for success were further complicated by the fact that there were no political parties at the time. From 1796 to 1816, there had been two parties, the Federalists and the

Republicans. But during the War of 1812, the Federalists had called on the New England states to secede from the Union. Only the signing of the Treaty of Ghent had kept them from going ahead with the idea. As a result, the Federalist Party had disappeared, and during Monroe's two presidential terms, every politician was assumed to be a Republican.

Without a party organization, how could presidential candidates campaign? For one thing, they did not campaign for themselves. It was not considered dignified. What each candidate had to do was to get the support of the leading newspapers and influential men in each state, and have them do the campaigning for him. Second, it would not have been physically possible. It is hard to cover much territory when the campaign trail consists of narrow dirt roads and slow-moving waterways.

In other words, the 1824 presidential election, unlike previous elections, was neither an unopposed succession nor a partisan struggle. Instead, it shaped up as a popularity contest. And that put Adams at a distinct disadvantage.

An Unpopular Man

John Quincy Adams was a brilliant statesman, probably the best secretary of state the United States has ever had. He negotiated the Treaty of Ghent, obtained Florida, and formulated the Monroe Doctrine. He was extremely hard-working, conscientious, honest, and principled. He could be charming and witty in a small group of friends. But he was not well liked. As one historian put it, "He alienated people almost without trying." He had developed chronic eye trouble, which made his eyes water all the time and gave him a shifty look. His manner was chilly, he did not shake hands well, and he was unable even to carry on a casual conversation.

A typical story tells how John Quincy Adams once met

an old farmer, who greeted him warmly. "Mr. Adams," he said, "my wife, when she was a gal, lived in your father's family; you were then a little boy, and she has often combed your head."

"Well, I suppose she combs yours now," John Quincy replied, thereby losing at least one vote.

Three Opponents

The three men who opposed Adams for the presidency were entirely different. All were popular, personable politicians. One came from the South, two from the West.

The southerner was Secretary of the Treasury William Crawford. He was a large, handsome man who gave out numerous offices to his friends. However, he suffered a stroke during the course of the campaign that left him half paralyzed and nearly blind. Although his supporters tried to keep the news quiet, Crawford's chances were considerably weakened.

That left the two westerners, Henry Clay and Andrew Jackson. A "war hawk" during the War of 1812, the tall, good-looking Clay had gone on to become Speaker of the House of Representatives. Adams described Clay as having "a vigorous intellect, an [eager] spirit, a handsome [way of speaking], though with a mind very defective in elementary knowledge, and a very indigested system of ethics."

The most popular figure was Jackson. Although he lacked a formal education, Jackson had practiced law successfully and had acquired considerable land and more than 100 slaves. He had also served as both a U.S. representative and a senator. Affectionately nicknamed "Old Hickory," he was best known as the hero of New Orleans and the conqueror of Florida. Reckless and full of life, with a commanding presence, Jackson stood in marked contrast to the short, bookish Adams.

PLAYING THE POLITICIAN

Adams faced a dilemma. On the one hand, he believed strongly that he was the logical successor to Monroe. On the other, he disapproved thoroughly of politics. He felt the office should seek the man, not vice versa. "If the people wish me to be President, I shall not refuse the office; but I ask nothing from any man." For Adams, his long record of public service was sufficient. If the only way to become President was by forming a political organization, "purchasing newspapers, bribing by appointments, or bargaining for foreign missions, I have no ticket in that lottery." Yet it was obvious that he would have to do something if he wanted to win the presidency.

So for the first—and last—time in his life, John Quincy Adams played the politician. He began by trying to get his opponents out of the country. First, he had Jackson named American minister to Mexico. But the general declined the offer. Next, he offered various ambassadorial posts to Clay, who also declined.

A Great Ball

John Quincy then threw a ball to celebrate the anniversary of both the Treaty of Ghent and the Battle of New Orleans. It was a grand affair and the highlight of the Washington social season.

The men wore their best blue coats, high white neckerchiefs, and silk stockings. The women carried fans and wore narrow silk gowns with jewels that shone brilliantly. Married women also wore turbans on their heads, as was the style of the times. There was dancing on the first floor until one o'clock in the morning, and a supper table on the third floor where people could eat "natural and candied fruits, pies,

This engraving of a ball given in 1824 by John Quincy Adams appeared in 1871 in a magazine called Harper's Bazaar. *Andrew Jackson stands in the center with his hand on his belt. Secretary of State and Mrs. Adams are shown on the far right.* (Library of Congress.)

sweetmeats, tongues, games, etc., prepared in French style, and arranged with most exquisite taste."

Louisa sent out 500 invitations – and nearly 1,000 guests showed up. As Adams wrote in his diary, "The crowd was great and the house could scarcely contain the company."

The purpose of the ball was to explore the possibility of an Adams-Jackson ticket: "John Quincy Adams, who can write, and Andrew Jackson, who can fight." Adams, of course, would be the presidential candidate, and Jackson would be the vice-presidential candidate. But although both men spent the evening being cordial to each other, no political partnership was formed.

Straddling the Fence

Adams then set out to woo the press. He gave interviews to as many reporters as possible. At the same time, he was careful not to express views that would antagonize any section of the country.

One campaign issue was the tariff. New England, anxious to encourage its industrial development, wanted a high protective tariff on manufactured goods, especially those from England. The South, whose economy depended on growing cotton, supported low tariff rates. Adams kept one foot in each camp by announcing that he favored a "cautious tariff," one that would reflect the federal government's "tender and sincere regard" for both sections of the country.

Another campaign issue was slavery. Adams was the only non-slaveholder among the presidential candidates. Furthermore, like almost all New Englanders, he disapproved of the institution, describing it in his diary as an "outrage upon the goodness of God" and a "great and foul stain upon the North

American Union." To reporters, however, he merely said that it was important to obey the laws. Southern readers were left free to assume that this included the laws upholding slavery.

THE HOUSE DECIDES

As the summer wore on, the campaign grew increasingly personal and nasty. Adams was criticized for his "English" wife and denounced as a snobbish aristocrat who preferred monarchy to democracy. Jackson was branded a murderer for having executed Arbuthnot and Armbrister in Florida. Clay was labeled a gambler and a drunkard. Crawford—who had considerable support in spite of his stroke—was accused of personal dishonesty. Charges and countercharges filled the newspapers, state legislatures issued endorsements, and supporters of the various candidates handed out pamphlets, delivered speeches, and canvassed for votes in taverns and religious meetings alike.

When the votes were counted, Jackson emerged as the popular choice, with more than 42 percent of the total as compared to Adams' 30 percent. Jackson also received the most electoral votes. But because he did not have a majority in the electoral college, the election was thrown into the House of Representatives. There, each state—of which there were now 24—would cast one vote.

Because Clay had received the fewest electoral votes of the four candidates, his name was dropped from consideration. Clay then threw his support to Adams. Clay had disliked Jackson for a long time. When Jackson invaded Florida, Clay spoke darkly of modern-day Caesars and Napoleons. He did not see how "killing Indians and fighting the British"

Henry Clay never won the presidency, but he served for many years in the U.S. Senate. There he became known as the Great Compromiser because of his attempts in 1820 and again in 1850 to balance the interests of North and South without breaking up the Union. (Library of Congress.)

made Jackson a good choice for the highest office in the land, especially when he had a violent temper and had killed several men in duels. Besides, Clay did not like the idea of a westerner other than himself becoming President of the United States.

Jousting for Support

All through January and early February, the Adams-Clay forces and the Jackson forces were busy arranging deals and lining up votes. Crawford, because of his stroke, was realistically out of the running. At last the day came. On February 9, 1825, the House of Representatives met to choose the next President.

As the balloting proceeded, it became clear that Adams had the votes of 12 states, one short of the number needed for election. The pivotal state was New York. But its delegation was split, and the man with the deciding vote was the aging and wealthy Stephen Van Rensselaer.

Van Rensselaer had originally supported Crawford but was now wavering between Crawford and Adams. As the ballot box neared him, he dropped his head on his desk and prayed for divine guidance. When he lifted his head, he saw a ballot on the floor by his seat. It bore the name of John Quincy Adams. Van Rensselaer put aside his Crawford ballot, picked up the "message from heaven," and voted for Adams.

That night, John Quincy Adams, sixth President-elect of the United States, wrote in his diary: "May the blessing of God rest upon the event of this day!" Then, ever honest, he added his disappointment over the way he had achieved his "destiny." He had hoped to be elected as "the man of all the people." Instead, he was only the choice of a group of politicians.

Dueling

Dueling became popular in the United States during the Revolutionary War and was widespread until after the Civil War, especially in the South. Most duels arose when one person insulted another, either verbally or in writing, usually by calling him a liar. Since everyone knew that a gentleman did not lie, the only way the insulted party could protect his honor and his reputation was by challenging the insulter to a duel. As Andrew Jackson put it, "The slanderer . . . [is] worse than the murderer."

The choice of weapons lay with the challenged man. Americans preferred pistols to swords or knives. However, because pistols in those days had a smooth rather than a rifled bore, they were not very accurate. As a result, most duels ended with nothing worse than powder burns for the two opponents. Occasionally, though, a dueler was wounded or even killed.

Andrew Jackson fought a famous duel in 1806 against a lawyer and sportsman named Charles Dickinson. Both men were Tennesseans. But because dueling was illegal in Tennessee, the duel took place across the state line in Kentucky. Jackson's behavior on this occasion was not as honorable as it should have been. When his pistol did not fire on his first try, he pulled the trigger again, even though that was against the rules. On another occasion, Jackson was challenged by someone he "knew not as a gentleman."

Jackson refused to duel. Instead, he suggested that the two men simply find a clearing in the forest and shoot it out informally. Henry Clay also took part in several duels. In 1809 Clay, who was then a member of the Kentucky state legislature, introduced several bills designed to protect new industries in the state. Humphrey Marshall accused Clay of being an unprincipled politician who cared more for manufacturers and businessmen than for farmers. Both Clay and Marshall were slightly wounded in the duel. But Clay made political capital out of it. He did not attend any legislative sessions for three weeks. This enabled his supporters to boast that their hero had ''fought and bled for the cause of protection.''

In 1825 Clay fought a duel against Senator John Randolph of Virginia. Randolph accused Clay of being a hypocrite and a 'scoundrel for his support of John Quincy Adams for President. In this duel, neither man was wounded, but a pistol shot damaged Randolph's cloak.

In 1839 John Quincy Adams, then a congressman from Massachusetts, co-sponsored a bill that imposed a heavy prison sentence on anyone in the District of Columbia who challenged another person to a duel or accepted such a challenge. Adams proposed the bill after a duel in which a representative from Maine was killed by a representative from Kentucky. In the course of the debate, Adams denounced dueling as a barbaric ''appendage [addition] to slavery.'' The antidueling bill became law in spite of southern opposition.

Chapter 7

The Second President Adams

John Quincy Adams – the only son of a President to become President himself – was inaugurated on March 4, 1825. He had slept hardly at all the two previous nights, and he faltered while delivering his inaugural address. Yet it was a skillful speech.

The new chief executive reviewed the tremendous growth of the country since the Constitution had been ratified. Its borders now stretched from the Atlantic Ocean to the Pacific Ocean, he reminded his audience. "The forest has fallen by the ax of our woodsmen; the soil has been made to teem with the tillage of our farmers; our commerce has whitened every ocean." Early disputes over government and foreign policy had been resolved, and the nation had been at peace for ten years. Adams appealed to the American people to stop squabbling, rise above party politics and sectional interests, and consider the welfare of the nation as a whole. He closed by asking for their indulgence of him as a minority President.

APPOINTING A CABINET

President Adams' first act was to select his Cabinet members. Although the New England states had provided the base for his election, none of his choices came from that region. In fact, most of his selections were political opponents. He offered to make Jackson secretary of war, and asked Crawford to remain as secretary of the treasury, but both men refused. Adams then filled the two posts with Crawford supporters, and also nominated a follower of his Vice-President, John C. Calhoun, as postmaster general.

Adams' most controversial appointment was that of Henry Clay as secretary of state. By experience and ability, Clay was unquestionably the most qualified man for the position. Also, Adams wanted a westerner to play a top role in his administration.

Political foes of Adams, however, felt certain the appointment was a payoff. Hadn't Adams and Clay met on a Sunday evening in January, a month before the election in the House, and held what Adams described in his diary as "a long conversation explanatory of the past and prospective of the future"? Hadn't Clay then proceeded to lobby mightily for Adams' election? Surely it was obvious the two men had made a "corrupt bargain." As Jackson asserted furiously: "The Judas of the West has closed the contract and will receive the thirty pieces of silver!"

Convinced he had been cheated out of the presidency, Jackson resigned from his seat in the U.S. Senate and was at once renominated for the presidency by the Tennessee legislature. And in Congress, his supporters swore to oppose Adams' program, whatever it might be.

A PROGRAM OF PUBLIC WORKS

During his first year in office, President Adams tried to find some great national project that would appeal to all Americans. He had always looked upon the United States as a nation rather than a group of states, and he strongly opposed the emphasis that Jackson and Calhoun put on states' rights.

Like many other politicians of the time, John C. Calhoun studied law before entering public life. He was a leading war hawk before the War of 1812 and served as Vice-President under both John Quincy Adams and Andrew Jackson. (Library of Congress.)

Adams believed in "liberty with power." Americans had won their liberty in the Revolution. Now the national government should use its power to promote the welfare of the people.

To Adams, this meant "internal improvements," or what is known today as public works. The national government,

Adams said, should build roads and canals to link the whole country together. It should organize a department of the interior to conserve and develop America's natural resources. It should set up a university to carry on scholarly research, and a naval academy to train officers for the U.S. Navy. It should establish a uniform standard of weights and measures. It should finance scientific explorations of the Northwest. It should build and equip an astronomical observatory, a "lighthouse of the sky." It should support the creative arts. In short, Adams felt it was the function of the national government to strengthen the country physically and intellectually.

Adams made the call for internal improvements the keynote of his first message to Congress. He pointed out that "foreign nations less blessed with . . . freedom" than America were "advancing with gigantic strides in the career of public improvement." If the United States did not do likewise, Adams argued, "would it not be to cast away the bounties of Providence, and doom ourselves to perpetual inferiority?"

In the 20th century, when the federal government does so much—from insuring the aged to sending astronauts to the moon—such proposals would be considered modest. But to Adams' dismay, his speech was greeted with mockery and suspicion. People hooted at the idea of "light-houses of the skies." They accused the President of being a monarchist because he had held up the example of "the nations of Europe and their rulers." He was just seeking power for himself, they said.

Sectional Fears

Rather than uniting the country, Adams' program of internal improvements managed to upset both the West and the South. He proposed paying for the program by increasing revenue from the sale of public lands. But since this would raise the

The Erie Canal was dug mostly by newly immigrated Irish "broadbacks." As many as 50 boats a day used the canal when it was completed. This view shows the canal near the town of Little Falls on the Mohawk River. (Library of Congress.)

The Erie Canal

The best-known internal improvement of John Quincy Adams' administration was the Erie Canal. Workers turned the first shovelful of earth in 1817. Eight years and $8 million later, the canal was opened to traffic.

The Erie Canal ran between the New York State capital of Albany, on the Hudson River, and Buffalo, on Lake Erie, a distance of about 350 miles. The canal was 4 feet deep and 40 feet wide at water level, tapering to 28 feet at the bottom. There were 83 locks, located wherever the ground rose or fell more than 6 or 7 feet.

Barges stayed in the middle of the canal. They were pulled by mules that walked on a towpath along one side of the canal. The reason mules were used instead of horses was that mules were sturdier. As one old-time canal skipper put it, ''When a mule got sick it either got well or died in four hours—you didn't need to send for the vet.'' With a speed limit of four miles an hour, the trip from one end of the canal to the other took 4½ days.

Originally, New York State officials had asked the federal government for money to build the waterway. But President Washington rejected the idea. So De Witt Clinton, the canal's biggest booster and later governor of New York, convinced the state legislature to fund the canal through nuisance taxes, such as a tax on salt and another on lotteries. In addition, private citizens bought canal bonds.

> The Erie Canal was an instant success. Goods could be shipped between Buffalo and New York City for one-tenth the cost of sending them by wagon. Grain and other agricultural products could move directly from the Great Lakes to the Atlantic Ocean. Settlers bound for Ohio, Michigan, Indiana, and Illinois could travel westward in relative comfort. New York, already the nation's largest city, soon became its busiest and richest seaport as well.
>
> The canalers who worked the barges were a rough and brawling lot. One of their favorite pastimes was playing jokes on passengers who were using the canal for the first time. The canalers would shout political slogans, such as "All Jackson men stand up." Then they would roar with laughter when the Jackson supporters stood up and were promptly knocked down by one of the low bridges that spanned the canal.

price of such land, it would make it harder for people who were moving westward to become independent farmers. Westerners promptly accused the President of trying to make people remain east of the Alleghenies, where they would form a cheap labor pool for eastern manufacturers.

The South feared the increased power of national government because they did not want it to interfere with the institution of slavery. As a result of the invention of the cotton gin, cotton had replaced tobacco and rice as the region's main money crop. Because growing cotton requires a great deal of labor, slavery became extremely profitable. Southern plantation owners were naturally very sensitive to antislavery feelings. They felt a strong national government would tackle the issue on a national basis. So southerners joined with westerners to oppose the President's program.

Adams' difficulties were not helped by his distaste for politics. To Adams, the only thing to consider when staffing the government was whether a person was competent. When Clay urged the President to fire an official in New Orleans because he was spreading vile rumors about Adams, the President refused. You did not fire a man for his opinions, he said. "Such a system would be repugnant to every feeling of my soul." The result was that the federal bureaucracy was filled with anti-Adams men. Similarly, when people who had supported Adams in the election asked him for jobs, they were turned away. As a result, there were no partisan groups to rally around the President and push his program.

Not one of Adams' proposals was enacted into law. As he wrote later, "I fell, and with me fell, I fear never to rise again in my day, the system of internal improvements by means of national energies. The great object of my life . . . has failed."

AN INEFFECTIVE PRESIDENT

Adams' political weakness showed in many other areas over the next four years. For example, in 1825 the eight newly independent nations of Latin America decided to hold a meeting in Panama. Because of the Monroe Doctrine, they invited the United States to attend. Adams thought it would be a good idea to send two commissioners. However, southern congressmen disagreed. The President was trying to involve the United States in entangling foreign alliances, they protested. Worse,

The White House stood only a short distance from John Quincy Adams' swimming hole in the Potomac river. The area was popular with fishermen as well as swimmers. (Library of Congress.)

he wanted to join with countries that had abolished slavery. That would set off slave revolts in the South! Although Congress eventually agreed to send the commissioners, they arrived too late to take part in the Panama meeting. Thus, an opportunity to create a working partnership between the United States and its southern neighbors was thrown away.

Again, in 1827, Georgia's governor was using the state militia to drive the Creek and Cherokee Indians from their lands. Although Adams considered Indians "an inferior species," he believed they should be treated fairly. Besides, the United States had a treaty with them. So Adams sent a message asking that federal troops be used to prevent the state militia from violating the treaty. But he had no political support—and the Creeks and Cherokees lost their land.

Life at the White House

As President, Adams kept up his usual intense routine. He would rise between five and six o'clock in the morning, dress, and go outdoors without bothering about breakfast. He took five-mile strolls around Washington, enjoyed listening to birdcalls, and sometimes went horseback riding in the countryside. In summer, he went swimming in the Potomac River. He did not bother with a bathing suit but simply peeled off his clothes and dove into the water.

Many stories were told about the President's swimming in the nude. According to one, someone stole Adams' clothes while he was in the water. When he emerged, he was forced to hide in a clump of bushes until a passing stroller could bring him fresh clothes from the White House. According to another story, a journalist named Mrs. Anne Royall, who published a Washington gossip sheet called *Paul Pry*, reportedly sat on his clothes until he answered her questions about banking and finance.

After his morning swim, Adams would return to the White House, read three chapters of the Bible, and go over papers on public business. After breakfast, he would receive a steady stream of visitors – department heads, foreign diplomats, office-seekers, and ordinary citizens. There was no Secret Service in those days and no screening of visitors. People simply walked into the White House and waited their turn to see the President. Adams often complained in his diary about the "nest of spiders." But once in a while he enjoyed his visitors, commenting on a woman seeking a position for her husband, "There is no pleader of this cause so eloquent as a young handsome woman and none who ought to be more firmly resisted." Dinner was served from five to half-past six, after which the President worked by the light of a kerosene lamp "in my chamber alone," doing paper work with the help of his secretarial staff: his son John. "Between eleven and twelve I retire to bed to rise again at five or six the next morning."

Apart from walking and swimming, Adams' only other relaxation was collecting acorns, seeds, and vines from his father's home in Quincy and transplanting them around the White House. Many of the oaks and catalpas that grace the White House lawn today were planted by the nation's sixth President.

THE CAMPAIGN OF 1828

The 1828 presidential election was a rematch between Adams and Jackson. It was not much of a contest, though. Even two years before the voting, it was clear that John Quincy Adams could not be re-elected. That year (1826), for the first time in the nation's history, the people chose a Congress that was overwhelmingly anti-administration in both houses. In addition, the followers of his former opponents, Jackson and Crawford, as well as those of his own Vice-President, Calhoun, formed a coalition to defeat him. This coalition would soon become a new political party, the Democratic Party.

The campaign between Adams and Jackson was marked by bitter personal attacks. Jackson supporters accused Adams of having stolen the 1824 election and thwarting the will of the people. Moreover, they charged, his administration was filled with incompetence and waste. They claimed Adams broke the Sabbath by going horseback riding on Sundays. In reality, he spent Sundays in church, often attending one service in the morning and another service at a different church in the afternoon.

Adams' opponents also accused him of squandering the people's money by buying a billiard table for the White House and billing the government for it. Actually, he paid the government back out of his own pocket: $50 for the table, $5 for the cues, and $6 for the billiard balls. And over and over, they attacked Adams for his supposed "corrupt bargain" with Clay.

The attacks on Jackson were equally shrill and nasty. He was accused of being, among other things, "an illiterate, a maniac, an atheist, and a slave trader." He had spent most of his life "in gambling, in cock-fighting, in horse-racing." He had used his position as governor of Florida to speculate in public lands. He had murdered six mutinous soldiers at New Orleans. Worst of all, he had married Rachel Jackson before she divorced her first husband. "Ought a convicted adulteress and her paramour husband to be placed in the highest offices of this free and Christian land?" asked one Adams pamphlet.

Driving Forces for Change

Never before had a presidential campaign been filled with such mud-slinging. However, the driving force behind the campaign was the radical changes sweeping the country. The common people were on the move. They wanted to do away with property qualifications for voting. They wanted to abolish imprisonment for debt. They wanted free public education. They wanted to work shorter hours than the customary sunup-to-sundown. How could a scholarly, aristocratic diplomat from the East be their leader? Their symbol was Andrew Jackson, a fighting frontiersman who had climbed the ladder of success without benefit of family or education.

Another driving force was the issue of slavery. Jackson was a slaveholder who had ruthlessly pursued fugitive slaves during his Florida campaign. Adams was from New England, and antislavery sentiment was rising in the North. The South, as well as the West, preferred Jackson to Adams.

A One-Term President

When the popular votes were counted, Jackson had 56 percent to 44 percent for Adams. The electoral college vote was more lopsided: 68 percent for Jackson to 32 percent for Adams. Like his father before him, John Quincy Adams was a one-term President.

Adams was crushed by the outcome. He had failed to gain his program of internal improvements, and he had been unable to unite the American people in a truly national government. It was "the ruin of our cause, the ruin of our administration." Moreover, the vicious campaign had left his "character and reputation a wreck." He was overcome by depression. Pains cramped his right side, he suffered from a severe cough, and he had trouble sleeping. "The sun of my political life sets in the deepest gloom," Adams lamented.

The transfer of power from Adams to Jackson was cold and impersonal. Jackson refused to follow custom and pay a courtesy call on his predecessor. His wife had died the month after the election, and Jackson felt that the campaign attacks by Adams' supporters were responsible for her death. For his part, Adams refused to attend Jackson's inauguration. Beaten and embittered, he prepared to leave Washington for Quincy, to "go into the deepest retirement and withdraw from all connections with public affairs."

Chapter 8

Congressman from Massachusetts

The year 1829 proved to be for John Quincy Adams his "furnace of affliction." It not only marked the end of his presidency, but it was also the year in which he lost his oldest son and most of his money.

PERSONAL DIFFICULTIES

John Quincy Adams had never been a successful father. He behaved toward his three sons as his own parents had toward him, only much more so. As one of the boys said, "Father doesn't talk to us, he lectures at us." Adams insisted that George, John, and Charles obtain a classical education with the aim of entering public service. If George preferred music and literature to politics and law, that was unfortunate but irrelevant. When John did better at sports than studies and failed to be among the top five of his class at Harvard, Adams refused to allow him to come home for Christmas. "My sons have not only their own honor but that of two preceding generations to sustain."

A Son Dies

The burden was too much for George. A gentle, dreamy young man, he had done well in school but seemed without direction after graduation. He was always falling into debt, calling on his father for help, promising to reform, and then falling into debt again. He also began drinking heavily, which did not help his law practice.

In April 1829, Charles wrote his parents that George was going to pieces. So the former President ordered his oldest son to come to Washington and help him and Louisa pack for their return to Quincy. George dutifully set out from Boston on the steamboat *Benjamin Franklin*. That evening, he went to bed with a violent headache but was unable to sleep. He suddenly felt afraid that other passengers were trying to break into his cabin, and that the ship's engines were talking to him. About an hour before sunrise, he rose and went on deck, where he spoke briefly with another passenger. A short time later, when the passenger returned to the place where he had talked with George, the young man was not there. Only his hat was lying on the deck. Two weeks later, George's body washed ashore on a beach along Long Island Sound.

To his parents, the apparent suicide of their oldest son was "a punishment from Heaven." Adams upbraided himself for urging George "to exertions foreign to his nature." Louisa was so shaken with grief that she became physically ill. It was left up to the former President to return alone to Quincy and fix up the old house he had inherited from his father.

It was about this time that Adams faced serious financial problems. He had invested most of his savings in some flour mills owned by one of Louisa's cousins. Unfortunately, the cousin was a poor manager. That, combined with storm damage to wheat fields and western competition, brought the mills to the edge of bankruptcy. Only several years of tireless effort by son John saved the former President from a debt-ridden old age.

A NEW CAREER

Adams gradually settled into a satisfying routine at Quincy. He had shelves built round his bedroom for his collection of books, probably the finest in the country. He started writing a biography of his father and also began making notes for a history of American political parties. He swam in the nearby creek and worked hard planting and pruning in the orchard. He was also elected to the Board of Overseers of Harvard University.

Then, in September 1830, the former President received a startling proposal from some local citizens. Would he run for Congress? The proposal was without precedent. The nation's first five former Presidents had all spent their declining years in respected retirement, occasionally delivering a ceremonial address but rarely, if ever, voicing an opinion on political issues.

Adams' family objected vigorously to the idea of his running for Congress. Louisa had been very happy to leave Washington, and felt that nothing good could come from her husband's "insatiable passion" for public office. Charles insisted that it would be highly undignified for a former chief executive to accept such a lowly post as member of the House of Representatives. It was like a general re-enlisting in the army as a private.

Adams thought otherwise. "No person [can] be degraded by serving the people," he said. He missed public life. Moreover, he feared that sectionalism was threatening the nation's unity, and he wanted to do what he could to prevent that from happening. As he wrote to Charles: "For myself, taught in the school of Cicero [a statesman of ancient Rome], I shall say, *Defendi respublicam adolescens; non deseram senex.* —'I will not desert in my old age the Republic that I defended in my youth.' "

So Adams accepted the nomination. Two months later, in November 1830, he won 75 percent of the vote against two opposition candidates. "I am a member-elect of the Twenty-Second Congress," he wrote jubilantly in his diary. "My election as President of the United States was not half so gratifying to my inmost soul." At the age of 63, Adams began his third public career.

"Independence and Union Forever!"

As a freshman congressman, Adams was appointed chairman of the House Committee on Manufactures. In this post, he played a major role in the struggle over the tariff.

In 1828 Congress had passed a protective tariff on imported manufactured goods. The tariff was so high that it was called the Tariff of Abominations. The state most affected by the tariff was South Carolina, the home state of Vice-President Calhoun. Accordingly, in 1831 Calhoun issued a statement in which he set forth the Theory of Nullification. Essentially, the theory held that a state could nullify, or set aside, any national law that hurt the state or that it considered to be unconstitutional. Furthermore, if the law was then passed by three-quarters of the states and became part of the Constitution, the injured state had the right to secede from the Union.

Adams disagreed strongly with this theory. True, the Constitution was originally an agreement among 13 states. But there were now 24 states, 11 of which had not been a party to the original agreement. In other words, there was now an American nation over and above any group of states.

The first part of the Smithsonian Institution was not completed until the 1840s. Unlike the classical style of Washington's other public buildings, the Smithsonian—built of red sandstone—was designed to resemble a Norman castle, with high towers and turreted walls. (Library of Congress.)

The Smithsonian Institution

In addition to being chairman of the Committee on Manufactures, John Quincy Adams was appointed chairman of a special House committee to decide whether to accept $500,000 that an English scientist named James Smithson had left to the United States "for the increase and diffusion of knowledge among men." Adams welcomed the gift and proposed building an observatory with the money. He still wanted an American "lighthouse of the sky." Southern congressmen objected, however. Setting up any sort of national educational institution, they said, would infringe on states' rights.

Adams then prepared a long report for Congress in which he pointed out that only humans, unlike birds and other animals, are capable of knowledge. "To furnish the means of acquiring knowledge is therefore the greatest benefit that can be conferred upon mankind. . . . To what higher and nobler object could this generous and splendid donation have been devoted?"

After two years, Adams convinced Congress to accept Smithson's legacy. But it took him eight more years of argument before Congress finally agreed, in 1846, to establish a national scientific museum called the Smithsonian Institution.

Today, the Smithsonian is a huge complex of some 14 museums, several art galleries, a zoo, a number of libraries and research institutes, a center for the performing arts—and even Adams' hoped-for observatory. The most popular of its museums is the National Air and Space Museum. It contains the Kitty Hawk Flyer of 1903, in which the Wright brothers made the world's first successful airplane flight. It also contains the Apollo II lunar command module *Columbia*, which carried three Americans into space for humankind's first landing on the moon in 1969.

The zoo is the only place in the country where there is a permanent exhibit of giant pandas from China. The observatory is headquartered in Adams' home state of Massachusetts. The Smithsonian also publishes two magazines, *Smithsonian* and *Air & Space/Smithsonian*, and produces a weekly radio program and several public television series on science and culture.

For his efforts on its behalf, John Quincy Adams was nicknamed "The Father of the Smithsonian Institution," an honor that he rightfully deserved.

And no state had the right to disobey a national law. Moreover, in Adams' view the United States was not a temporary association of states but a permanent one. Once a state joined the Union, it could not leave.

The former President expressed his beliefs in a Fourth of July speech in 1831 at the Quincy town meeting. The Declaration of Independence, Adams asserted, was an agreement between citizens and their government in which "union was as vital as freedom or independence." Nullification was nothing "more nor less than treason." He closed with the rallying cry, "Independence and Union forever!" The audience broke into cheers, and 2,000 copies of the speech were printed and sent to important men around the country.

A Firebrand in the House

The next year, 1832, Adams' Committee on Manufactures reported out a tariff bill that lowered many rates, especially the rate on the rough cloth used to make clothing for slaves. Almost everyone thought the new law was a great improvement over the Tariff of Abominations—everyone, that is, except Calhoun. To him, any protective tariff at all was reason for nullification. So later that year, South Carolina called a convention that declared the Tariff of 1832 "null, void, and no law" within its borders. The convention added that if the federal government tried to collect tariff duties in Charleston and other ports, South Carolina would declare itself independent.

To Adams' pleased surprise, President Jackson did not go along with his fellow slaveholders. Instead, he called on Congress to pass a Force Bill, giving him the authority to use federal troops to put down any resistance in South Carolina. But at the same time, he asked that tariff rates be lowered still further.

As Congress debated the legislation, Adams grew increasingly angry. Why should slaveholders be a "privileged class of citizens?" If they called in federal troops whenever a slave revolt broke out, on what ground did they oppose the use of federal troops to enforce a federal law? And why should they be rewarded with lower tariff rates because they threatened to secede?

Then a representative from Georgia rose to speak. "Slaves sail the Northern ships and run the Northern spindles," he said accusingly. *"Our slaves are our machinery*, and we have as good a right to profit by them as do the Northern men to profit by the machinery they employ."

That was too much for Adams. Machinery indeed! "That 'machinery,' " he observed, "sometimes exerts self-moving power." He was referring to a slave rebellion that occurred in 1831. He continued: "My constituents possess as much right to say to the people of the South, 'We will not submit to the protection of your interests,' as the people of the South have the right to address such language to them." In other words, if South Carolina could nullify a tariff, then Massachusetts could refuse to help slaveowners control their slaves and recapture fugitives.

"The member from Massachusetts has thrown a firebrand into the Hall," shouted a congressman from South Carolina. "It is not I who have thrown the 'firebrand,' " retorted Adams. "The Nullification Ordinance is the firebrand."

After a few more angry speeches, things quieted down. Congress passed both the Force Bill and the Tariff of 1833. South Carolina then repealed the Nullification Ordinance. Both sides claimed victory. But Adams was more aware than ever that the issue of slavery was indeed threatening the nation's unity.

THE SLAVERY ISSUE

Slavery had always been a troublesome matter for the country. For example, at the start of the Revolutionary War, when John Quincy was just eight years old, a group of Boston slaves had offered to fight on the side of the British in exchange for their freedom. Adams remembered what his mother had written his father. "I wish most sincerely that there was not a slave in the province. It always appeared a most [wicked] scheme to me — to fight ourselves for what we are daily robbing and plundering from those who have as good a right to freedom as we have."

The Missouri Compromise

When the U.S. Constitution was drawn up in 1787, most of the delegates to the convention wanted to abolish slavery. But Georgia and South Carolina refused to join the Union if that happened. So nothing was done. By 1804, however, all the northern states had abolished slavery. On the other hand, with the invention of the cotton gin, slavery became an even more important part of southern life.

In the meantime, the United States was growing. And each time a new state applied for admission, a political battle erupted in Congress. Southern representatives demanded that the new state come in as a slave state. Northern representatives insisted that it come in free. The battle grew so fierce that a compromise had to be worked out. Under the Missouri Compromise of 1820, Maine was admitted as a free state and Missouri as a slave state, keeping the balance of slave and free states in the Senate at 12 and 12. However, it was agreed that in the future, slavery was to be prohibited in all states carved out of the Louisiana Territory north of 36°30′ north latitude.

A Presidential Wish

As secretary of state at that time, Adams did not comment publicly on the Missouri Compromise. Nor did he voice his feelings during the presidential election of 1824, for he did

A slave has his chains struck from his wrists as he leaves a slave state for a free state. Slave-owners were usually pictured with whips and dogs. (Library of Congress.)

not want to lose any more southern votes than he had to. As chief executive, he saw to it that the constitutional provisions dealing with slavery were carried out. But he felt strongly that compromises on the issue were bound to break down. Eventually, Adams believed, southern planters would secede from the Union, the slaves would revolt, and after a civil war, a new and stronger United States would come into being.

Adams even composed a sonnet on the matter, writing it in shorthand so that it could not be read by strangers. The last verse was as follows:

> That nature's God commands the slave to rise,
>   And on the oppressor's head to break his chain.
> Roll, years of promise, rapidly roll round,
> Till not a slave shall on this earth be found.

The Abolitionist Movement

About the time Adams was elected to the House of Representatives, the abolitionist movement to abolish slavery in the country began gathering strength in the North. Adams himself favored gradual abolition. The abolitionist movement, on the other hand, wanted to free all slaves immediately.

The abolitionists used various methods to promote their cause. They held meetings at which fugitive slaves described the evils of slavery. They published newspapers. They distributed pamphlets. They organized some 2,000 antislavery societies. And especially, they bombarded the House of Representatives with petitions in order to encourage public debate on the issue.

The Right of Petition

One of Adams' first acts as a congressman was to present 15 petitions asking Congress to abolish slavery in the District of Columbia. Adams himself disagreed with the idea. He believed the District's residents, rather than Congress, should be the ones to take such action. However, the First Amendment to the Constitution guaranteed citizens the right to petition their government "for redress of grievances." So he presented the petitions.

Congress took no action on the issue over the next three years. However, the number of petitions that Adams presented every Monday morning grew by leaps and bounds as the abolitionists increased their activities.

In the meantime, southerners began to clamp down on any discussion of their "peculiar institution," as slavery was called. They closed the mails in the South to abolitionist literature. Anyone found distributing it was jailed or whipped. Louisiana declared it a crime to say anything "from bar, bench or stage" that might "produce discontent" among slaves. Mobs in such border states as Missouri smashed the presses of antislavery publishers.

By 1834 southerners were turning their attention northward. The governor of Virginia wrote to the governor of Massachusetts demanding that he suppress *The Liberator*, a leading abolitionist newspaper. The mayor of Savannah, Georgia, wrote to the mayor of Boston insisting that he imprison David Walker, a free black who was calling on slaves to revolt.

The Gag Rule

Finally, in 1836, Representative Henry Laurens Pinckney of South Carolina introduced three resolutions in Congress. The first stated that Congress had no constitutional power to interfere with slavery in the states. The second stated that Congress had no constitutional power to interfere with slavery in the District of Columbia. The third stated that in the future, all petitions concerning slavery or its abolition should automatically be tabled, or set aside, "without being either printed or referred [to a committee] . . . and that no further action whatever shall be had thereon."

Adams reacted at once. To him, the "gag rule" was a clear violation of the First Amendment. Over and above the issue even of slavery, such a rule would stifle free speech and the right of petition. It must not be allowed.

So the frail, rheumatic, 70-year-old former President with trembling hands and runny eyes rose to his feet and joined battle. It was a battle he would continue to fight, one way or another, for the rest of his life.

Chapter 9

Defeats and Victories

For the next 12 years, John Quincy Adams walked "on the edge of a precipice." His aim was to force a public debate on slavery without splitting the Union. His method was a flanking strategy. Instead of attacking slavery head-on, Adams fought against the gag rule. In that way, he gained the support of those who were unconcerned about slavery but who valued the rights Americans had fought for in the Revolutionary War—freedom of speech and of petition.

PASSAGE OF THE GAG RULE

Adams began by resisting Pinckney's three resolutions. After several southern congressmen had spoken in favor of the resolutions, Adams tried to gain the floor in order to speak in opposition. But the House Speaker—a slaveholder from Tennessee—ignored him, and the House voted to cut off further debate.

"Am I gagged or am I not?" shouted the former President.

He was, but he did not let that stop him. After the House approved the first resolution—that Congress not interfere with slavery in the states—it took up a different matter: relief to white southern refugees from the Seminole Wars. Since the matter was considered uncontroversial, the Speaker recognized Adams. The former President promptly extended his remarks to the broader topic of Congress' war powers. Adams warned about the possibility of civil war. If there were a slave uprising in the South, he asserted, "from that instant the war powers of Congress extend to interference with the institution of slavery in every way by which it can be interfered with."

Hardly anyone paid much attention, though. Pinckney's second resolution—that Congress not interfere with slavery in the nation's capital—was approved, with Adams abstaining. Then the clerk began calling the roll on the third resolution, the gag rule. Adams' name was first. Instead of saying yes or no, he rose and shouted: "I hold the resolution to be in direct violation of the Constitution of the United States, of the rules of this House, and of the rights of my constituents." He then demanded that the clerk record his statement in the official *Register of Debates*. The clerk ignored the demand. Pinckney's third resolution passed, 117 to 68, and the gag rule was adopted.

PARLIAMENTARY MANEUVERS

From then on, Adams used every method he could think of to bring the issue of slavery before Congress. Since every session of Congress makes its own rules, there were always a few days at the start of each congressional session when the gag rule was not in effect. At such times, Adams presented petitions by the dozen. One day he reached a peak of 350.

Adams always followed the same procedure, which was designed to needle his opponents. He would present one petition at a time. The Speaker would order the petition tabled without being read. Adams would then move that the petition be read first. The Speaker would rule Adams out of order. Adams would appeal the Speaker's decision to the House. The House would uphold the Speaker.

And so it went, with southern congressmen growing angrier and angrier at Adams' persistence. Sometimes their grumblings and catcalls drowned out what he was saying. He was a "madman from Massachusetts," a "hell-hound of abolition." Adams responded by mockingly labeling southern plantation owners as "the Slavocracy."

A Questionable Petition

At times Adams was able to trick his opponents. One such incident took place in February 1837. Adams asked the Speaker to issue a ruling. He had a petition signed with "scrawls and marks" that apparently came from slaves. Could he present it?

As the *Register of Debates* put it, there was *"Great consternation in the House!"* No petition from slaves had ever come before Congress. One southern representative after another jumped to his feet to denounce Adams. He was a pawn of "incendiary fanatics." He was inciting slaves to rebellion and should be indicted for doing so. He was offending the South. He was threatening the Union. "Expel him! Expel him!"

Finally, a congressman introduced a motion for censure (an official reprimand); it was seconded, and debate on it began. A point of order, said Adams. In the first place, he had not actually presented the petition. He had merely asked if he could. Secondly, the censure motion should be thrown out because it described the petition as being opposed to slavery, whereas in fact it called for the *retention* of slavery. The second uproar in the House was even greater than the first. This time, two motions were made. The first stated that slaves did not have the right to present petitions. The second sought to censure Adams for having deliberately fooled the House of Representatives and trampled on its dignity.

An Outstanding Speech

Adams' speech in his defense was one of the finest of his career. "There is not a word in the Constitution of the United States excluding petitions from slaves," he declared. He continued: "The framers of the Constitution would have repudiated the idea that they were giving to the people the right of petition. No, Sir. That right God gave to the whole human race when he made them *men* – the right of prayer, by asking a favor of another." He further pointed out, "No despot of any age or clime has ever denied this humble privilege to the poorest or the meanest of human creatures." There was silence in the House as Adams cried, "When you begin to limit the right, where shall it stop?"

As for those who accused him of tricking the House and threatened him with indictment, Adams bitingly suggested that "they should first be careful to pay attention to the facts." Then he thundered indignantly: "Did the gentleman think he could frighten me from my purpose by his threat of a grand jury? If that was his object, let me tell him *he mistook his man*. I am not to be frightened from the discharge of a duty by the indignation of the gentleman from South Carolina, nor by all the grand juries of this universe!"

Taken aback, Adams' opponents tried to withdraw the

motions but without success. They succeeded in passing the motion denying slaves the right to petition. But the motion censuring Adams was defeated by a resounding vote of 105 to 21.

From then on, Adams received threatening letters from southerners almost every day. One such letter pictured him with a bullet hole in his head. Another bore a drawing in red of a fist clutching a knife. Beneath it was a caption reading, "Vengeance is mine, say the South!" A third letter, which carried a skull and crossbones on top, informed the former President that a lynch mob was coming to Washington "to string him up from the highest oak on the grounds of the National Capitol." Adams calmly observed that such attitudes were just what one might expect from the mentality of slaveowners. He continued his fight.

THE QUESTION OF TEXAS

The fight soon shifted to a different matter. The Lone Star Republic of Texas, newly independent from Mexico, applied for admission to the United States.

Adams found himself pulled in two directions. On the one hand, he was a long-time believer in Manifest Destiny. He had supported the Louisiana Purchase even though it had cost him his Senate seat. As secretary of state, he had expanded the nation's boundaries through the acquisition of Florida and the signing of the Transcontinental Treaty with Spain. He had even offered to buy Texas from Mexico when he was President.

On the other hand, Adams had justified this empire-building as the expansion of democracy into new territory.

And that no longer applied to Texas. One of the clauses in its constitution overturned Mexico's law abolishing slavery. It also prohibited the Texas legislature from ever freeing the slaves in the area. Furthermore, it seemed likely that four or five slave states would be carved out of Texas. That would upset the balance of free and slave states in the Senate and would give the South a strong majority in both houses of Congress. It might even lead to war with Mexico, which was bound to resent America's takeover of its former province.

"And again I ask, what would be your *cause* in such a war?" thundered Adams. "Aggression, conquest, and the reestablishment of slavery where it had been abolished. In that war, sir, the banners of *freedom* will be the banners of Mexico; and your banners, I blush to speak the word, will be the banners of slavery."

Despite Adams' stirring words, Congress agreed in late 1837 to recognize the Lone Star Republic. But he had aroused so much public opinion against annexation that in 1838 Texas withdrew its application for statehood.

THE *AMISTAD* CASE

In 1841 the fight against slavery shifted to a different arena: the Supreme Court of the United States. It involved a case known as the *Amistad* case.

Two years earlier, some 52 African blacks had been kidnapped from Africa and transported to Cuba. There they were purchased by two Spanish slave traders named José Ruiz and Pedro Montez, who jammed them into the schooner *Amistad* for shipment to a sugar cane plantation. The entire procedure was illegal. Spain had not only outlawed the slave trade,

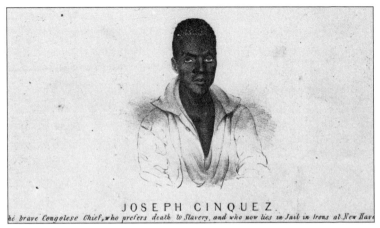

JOSEPH CINQUEZ.
he brave Congolese Chief, who prefers death to Slavery, and who now lies in Jail in Irons at New Have

Abolitionists distributed copies of Cinqué's statement that "It is better to die than be a white man's slave" throughout the North. Ironically, after returning to Africa, Cinqué enslaved the tribe that had killed his wife and sold him into slavery. (Library of Congress.)

it had also passed a law saying that any slaves imported into a Spanish colony, which Cuba was, were to be freed immediately.

On the fifth day out of Havana, the blacks aboard the *Amistad*, led by a man named Cinqué, rebelled. They killed most of the crew but spared the two slave traders on condition that they steer the *Amistad* back to Africa. Ruiz and Montez steered east by day but northwest by night, hoping to reach a southern U.S. port. Instead, the ship ended up in Long Island Sound, where it was taken into custody by a U.S. naval vessel. The blacks were jailed and charged with murder.

The resulting case contained all sorts of legal technicalities. The basic outcome hinged on whether the blacks were slaves or free men who had been illegally kidnapped. If they were slaves, they were guilty of murder and had to be turned over to Spanish authorities for punishment. It they were free men, the killings were in self-defense, and the United States was obligated to send them back to Africa.

Abolitionists formed a "Committee of Friends of the *Amistad* Africans" and hired lawyers to plead the case. They won the decision and also the first appeal. Then the case was appealed a second time, to the U.S. Supreme Court. At that point the Committee of Friends asked Adams – a recognized expert on international law – to join the argument for the defense.

Adams was reluctant at first. "I am too old, too oppressed by my duties in the House of Representatives, too inexperienced after a lapse of thirty years in the forms and technicalities of arguments before the Supreme Court." But how could he say no?

So on February 23, 1841, John Quincy Adams appeared before the Supreme Court and spoke for four hours – without notes. On March 1 he spoke for an additional three hours – again without notes. Adams argued that the Africans should not be considered slaves because the international slave trade had already been outlawed by treaty. Therefore, the fugitive slave laws of the United States – which required that fugitive slaves be returned to their owners – did not apply. In fact, Adams proclaimed, the only "crime" Cinqué and the other blacks had committed was the same "crime" that Adams' father and thousands of other Americans had committed during the Revolutionary War – the crime of fighting against those who sought to enslave them.

Supreme Court Justice Joseph Story commented that Adams' argument was "extraordinary, for its power, for its bitter sarcasm, and its dealing with topics far beyond the record and points of discussion." And on March 9, by a vote of six to one, the *Amistad* Africans were declared free.

A New-Found Popularity

As the 1840s continued, something wonderful happened to John Quincy Adams. As a consequence of his fight against slavery, he found himself a popular man for the first time in his life.

For example, in the summer of 1843, he went on a sightseeing trip to Canada and Niagara Falls with his daughter-in-law and his eldest grandson. When he re-entered the United States at Buffalo, New York, he was welcomed by thousands of people. "Crowds of people were assembled, received me with three cheers, and [showed] a desire to see and hear me."

In late fall, Adams was chosen to lay the cornerstone of the nation's first astronomical observatory in Cincinnati, Ohio. The trip turned out to be a triumphal journey. Every place he stopped, cannons fired, bells rang, and fireworks brightened the night sky. In Erie, Pennsylvania, he was given a torchlight parade. In Akron, Ohio, a "very pretty" young woman kissed the 76-year-old former President on the cheek. Adams promptly "returned the salute on the lip, and kissed every woman that followed, at which some made faces but none refused." At Columbus, Ohio, he had an escort of two companies of soldiers and a brass band. In Cincinnati, a banner reading "John Quincy Adams, the Defender of the Rights of Man" was strung across the main street. Bands and processions met him at Covington and Maysville, Kentucky. Everywhere, he was greeted with enthusiasm and affection.

Repeal of the Gag Rule

By now, Adams had been fighting for the right of petition for eight years. Each year he moved to have the gag rule repealed, and each year he lost. However, the margin of votes against him had been dwindling, from 49 in 1837 to just 3 in 1843.

In April 1844, Adams received a gift from a group of admirers. It was an ivory cane tipped with silver and inlaid with a gold American eagle. In the eagle's beak was a scroll with the motto "Right of Petition Triumphant" and a blank space for the date when the gag rule would be repealed. Because Adams always refused to accept gifts, he turned the cane over to the Patent Office for safekeeping.

On December 3, 1844, Adams introduced his usual resolution to allow antislavery petitions to be presented to Congress. This time it carried by a vote of 105 to 80. The margin of victory was supplied by a group of disgruntled Democratic congressmen whose candidate for President had been rejected in favor of James Knox Polk, a slaveholder. What better way to get revenge than by voting against the gag rule, which Polk supported?

John Quincy Adams was ecstatic nonetheless. "Blessed, forever blessed, be the name of God!" the former President wrote in his diary. He retrieved the cane from the Patent Office and engraved the date on it. Then he presented it to "the people of the United States."

Chapter 10

"At the Post of Duty"

John Quincy Adams was now 76 years old. He suffered from a continual cough. He was no longer strong enough to go swimming, and he had to ride in a carriage to the Capitol instead of walking. His hand shook so much that he had to use a metal support while writing. "I approach the term when my daily journal must cease from physical disability to keep it up. . . . I rose this morning at four, and with smarting, bloodshot eye and shivering hand, still sat down and wrote to fill up the chasm of the closing days of the last week; but my stern chase after Time is . . . like the race of a man with a wooden leg after a horse."

Nevertheless, Adams continued in his "unbearable labors" in the House. He attended sessions regularly, was punctual to the minute, and, as always, did not hesitate to speak his mind.

A WAR BEGINS

In January 1845, the administration again asked Congress to annex Texas. Ordinarily the matter would have taken the form of a treaty. But the administration did not have the necessary two-thirds majority in the Senate to approve a treaty. So it presented the matter as a joint resolution, which needed only a simple majority in both houses.

This daguerrotype of John Quincy Adams is believed to be the first photograph ever taken of a U.S. President. It was made in 1848 in Adams' Massachusetts home. (The Metropolitan Museum of Art, Gift of I. N. Phelps Stokes, Edward S. Hawes, Alice Mary Hawes, Marion Augusta Hawes, 1937.)

Once again, Adams tried to prevent annexation. In his opinion, it would lead to a war of conquest against Mexico, which in turn would lead to the breakup of the Union. "The spirit of freedom and the spirit of slavery are drawing together for the deadly conflict of arms." He would change his mind, he said, only under two conditions: "I am still willing to take Texas without slavery *and with the assent of Mexico.*" But a combination of southerners and expansionists carried the resolution in the House by 120 to 98, and the Senate agreed. "The heaviest calamity that ever befell myself and my country was this day consummated," Adams wrote in his diary.

As Adams had predicted, the Mexican-American War broke out in the spring of 1846 after a series of border incidents. Only 13 congressmen joined him in voting against "the most unrighteous war." Adams explained his position in a letter to Albert Gallatin, who had been one of his fellow negotiators at Ghent. The movement of American troops into disputed border territory was, Adams felt, an act of war taken without the consent of Congress. The Constitution had given the war powers to Congress, and a President had no right to take them away. "It is not difficult to foresee what the ultimate issue will be to the people of Mexico," Adams commented sadly, "but what it will be to the people of the United States, is beyond my foresight, and I turn my eyes away from it."

DECLINING YEARS

A few weeks later, while in Boston, Adams suffered a cerebral stroke. For a few days, he lay paralyzed, but then gradually recovered the full use of his body. In February 1847, when he again entered the halls of Congress for the first time since his stroke, he received an unexpected welcome. Proceedings stopped and every man rose, applauding loudly as two congressmen escorted the former President to his seat. He was no longer the "madman from Massachusetts" but "Old Man Eloquent," respected even by those who disagreed with what he said.

By now Adams was too weak to serve on any committee except one supervising the Library of Congress. Still, he attended congressional sessions regularly and voted in the roll calls. He voted for a peace with Mexico without any territorial concessions by either country. His side lost, and the United States gained 850,000 square miles of land, including what is now California, Nevada, and Utah, as well as parts of Arizona, Colorado, and New Mexico. Adams also voted against a resolution to award $50,000 to the owners of the *Amistad* for the loss of their "slaves." This time, his side won.

On July 27, 1847, the former President and his wife celebrated their 50th wedding anniversary. Their second son, John, had died some years earlier, and only Charles remained. However, there were nine grandchildren, five boys and four girls, to carry on the Adams name and family tradition.

The Last Days

The new year of 1848 seemed to bring new vigor to the 80-year-old Adams. He attended a reception given by the mayor of Washington. He and Louisa held an open house for hundreds of guests. As always, he went to church twice each Sunday. And he and his wife made plans to attend an upcoming ball in honor of George Washington's birthday.

On February 21, Adams was in his seat in the House. The first item of business was a motion to award medals to some of the generals who had fought in the Mexican-American War. Adams scowled. The war, in his opinion, had been un-

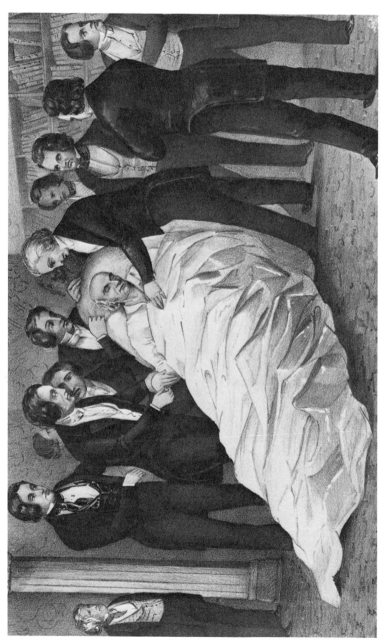

A small bronze plaque at the U.S. Capitol marks the spot where Adams suffered his fatal stroke. He died less than three years after his old rival, Andrew Jackson. (Library of Congress.)

necessary and unconstitutional, and he was certainly not going to thank those who had waged it.

When the first roll call came, he replied "No!" in a firm, clear voice. A few minutes later, the second roll call began. Suddenly, a reporter seated at the press table noticed Adams' face turning a deep red. He clutched the side of his desk. Then he slumped to his left. The congressman at the adjoining desk jumped up and caught the former President before he fell to the floor. "Mr. Adams is dying! Mr. Adams is dying!" the congressman cried out.

The former President was carried into the Speaker's room and placed on a sofa. He revived briefly and called for Henry Clay, who came, weeping, to hold his hand. A little later Adams murmured: "This is the end of earth, but I am composed," and sank into a coma. Two days later, on February 23, 1848, he died.

The following day, all the members of Congress, southerners as well as northerners, gathered to pay their respects. The House Speaker expressed the general feeling:

A seat on this floor has been vacated, towards which all eyes have been accustomed to turn with uncommon interest.

A voice has been hushed forever, to which all ears have been wont to listen with profound reverence.

He has been privileged to die at his post; to fall while in the discharge of his duties; and expire beneath the roof of the Capitol.

After a week of mourning, Adams' body was taken to Quincy, where he was buried beside his parents. Guns boomed a salute from the rocky ledge on top of Penn's Hill where the eight-year-old John Quincy had sat and watched the Battle of Bunker Hill. A placard read: "John Quincy Adams. Born a citizen of Massachusetts. Died a citizen of the United States."

Bibliography

Clarke, Fred. *John Quincy Adams*. New York: Macmillan, 1966. A vivid, informative text that paints a compelling picture of our sixth President and provides many details on the workings of the American government.

Falkner, Leonard. *For Jefferson and Liberty: The United States in War and Peace, 1800–1815*. New York: Alfred A. Knopf, 1972. A well-written history of the period, based on contemporary accounts, with information on such topics as impressment, the Louisiana Purchase, and the War of 1812.

Hoyt, Edwin P. *John Quincy Adams*. Chicago: Reilly & Lee, 1963. A fine biography that recreates the era in which our sixth President lived and explains the origin of political parties.

Lomask, Milton. *John Quincy Adams: Son of the American Revolution*. New York: Farrar, Straus & Giroux, 1965. A well-written biography that stresses Adams' family background and dramatically describes the *Amistad* case.

Meltzer, Milton. *Bound for the Rio Grande: The Mexican Struggle, 1845–1850*. New York: Alfred A. Knopf, 1974. A description of the causes, events, and results of the Mexican-American War, filled with excerpts from such original sources as diaries, letters, songs, newspaper accounts, and speeches of the day.

Scott, John Anthony. *Hard Trials on My Way: Slavery and the Struggle Against It, 1800–1860.* New York: Alfred A. Knopf, 1974. A vivid account of life in the slave South and of the struggle against slavery, based on contemporary diaries, letters, songs, and speeches, including some by slaves.

Index